TRADITIONS MYTHS & MEMORIES

1693 · 1993

CELEBRATING THE TERCENTENARY

• *Of* •

THE COLLEGE OF WILLIAM & MARY

In Virginia

Unfold the rich tapestry of history.
Tell a tale. Spin a story.
Speak of beginning and building,
of learning and of coming "home"
. . . of traditions, myths
and memories.

Christmas '95
from Rebecca

TRADITIONS MYTHS & MEMORIES

1693 · 1993

CELEBRATING THE TERCENTENARY

· *Of* ·

THE COLLEGE OF WILLIAM & MARY

In Virginia

Narrative by Wilford Kale

Graphic Design by Greta Matus

Primary Photography by C. James Gleason

Acknowledgements

Imagine a family of more than 70,000 members sifting through three hundred years worth of history. Summarizing William and Mary's three centuries of traditions, myths and memories has been something like that. Such a mammoth—and rewarding—challenge would not have been possible without the efforts and contributions of numerous people.

The Society of the Alumni would like to acknowledge the contributions of the following:
Barry Adams, executive vice president of the Society of the Alumni, for his initiation and support of the project, Wilford Kale '66 for narrative, Greta Matus for concept and design, C. James Gleason for primary photography, S. Dean Olson for coordinating the project, Virginia Carter Collins '77 for research and editing, Pam Kirschbaum for editing, Charles L. Kendrick '82 for marketing, Mary Ann Williamson for desktop publishing, Sylvia Colston for composition, Stephanie Westdyke for proofreading, Elizabeth Cobbledick, Jennifer L. Hughes '92, Ben F. Kellam '78 and John Freeman for support.

Additional photography was provided by
Jack Mellot, Tim Wright, Tony Sylvestro, Dan Dry, Carol Glover, Barbara Ball, Lyle Rosbotham '71, William K. Geiger '77, Kennett S. Bennett '87 and the late Jean Wyckoff Gwaltney '56.

Other photos were provided by
M. Carl Andrews '27, Agnes '31 and Davis Y. Paschall '32, Wilford Kale '66, the Muscarelle Museum of Art, W. Samuel Sadler '64, the Society of the Alumni and the archives at Earl Gregg Swem Library.

Special thanks to the alumni who contributed those memories that make this such a special reflection of William and Mary through the ages —memories that indeed "knit the generations each to each."
Richard F. Abrahamson '70, Alvin P. Anderson '70, '72 J.D., M. Carl Andrews '27, Robert S. Andrialis '65, William A. Armbruster '57, Houston Ashworth '41, Joanna Lee Ashworth '84, Elaine Campton Baker '49, James W. Baker '51, Henretta Trent Band '54, Joan Eastman Bennett, J. D. Bowers '89, Ira B. Dworkin '43, '48 B.C.L. John S. Entwisle '44, William D. Eppes '39, Lisa Beth Flechner '90, Chester F. Giermak '50, Milton Greenblatt '43, Frances L. Grodecoeur '39, Gladys Bennett Guy '24, Jane Speakman Hauge '38, Susan Arnot Heaney '79, Jeanne Lull Hopke '80, Warren P. Joblin '60, Elaine Elias Kappel '55, Elizabeth W. Lanier '30, Margaret Peck Latham '41, Mary Sowell League '80, Andrew J. Madigan '91, Virginia Lee McAlinden '45, Harriet Council Mead '35, Thomas M. Mikula '48, Margaret Mitchell Mollenkopf '41, Lucy Venable Jones Murphy '48, Peter Neufeld '58, Davis Y. Paschall '32, William T. Prince '55, Keith C. Reagan '88, James C. Rees '74, Margaret Mary Parmelee Sheridan '35, C. Malcolm Sullivan '42, Harry Tanzer '49, Stewart A. Tatem '89, William G. Thompson, Jr. '28, Ginnie Peirce Volkman '64, Raymond T. Waller '40, Winfred O'Neil Ward '54, Dick Weber '65, Natalie Hill Zung '69.

TRADITIONS, MYTHS & MEMORIES:
Celebrating the Tercentenary of the College of William and Mary in Virginia

The Society of the Alumni
The College of William and Mary in Virginia

Printed in Hong Kong
Four Colour Imports
Louisville, Kentucky

Library of Congress Catalog Card Number: 92-72780
ISBN 0-9615670-2-3

Introduction

There is something about this historic institution that allows the traditions of three hundred years to blend with the events of today in a happy, almost spiritual feeling. For without traditions, the College of William and Mary in Virginia would be just another state-supported school in a long list of nationally known colleges and universities.

But William and Mary is distinctive. Its heritage is warm and rich and its traditions are numerous and important.

Traditions—in the broadest sense—are doctrines and customs of strong historic significance transmitted from generation to generation. Traditions also can be created with each succeeding generation. Memories, on the other hand, are those recollections and reminiscences that can be remembered by an individual. And myths. They may or may not be true but often are remembered.

Until 1901 the eighteenth-century "Spotswood Cannon" was not a part of William and Mary lore. It was not a tradition. It was given at that time to the College by alumni from Brunswick County. According to a combination of William and Mary history and myth, the cannon was cast in 1713 for Fort Christiana, built by Governor Alexander Spotswood, from whom the cannon draws its name. The weapon was uncovered at the fort and later erected in front of the Wren Building, near the statue of Lord Botetourt. It stands today as a symbolic sentinel. In January 1986, Old Spotswood was removed, purportedly until a new carriage could be built, but it was 20 months before it was returned and not until alumni began to protest its absence.

A tradition almost vanished, like the "William and Mary Victory March" played after every touchdown. The song now is rarely heard, vanished from the band's repertoire in the 1980s, and most alumni don't even know of its existence. Other traditions, such as bowing to Lord Botetourt or tipping a duc hat as freshmen passed the statue, ceased when Botetourt was moved.

Myths include the assembling on the second floor of the library of a complete Model-T Ford, the firing of the Spotswood Cannon at the President's House, the successful culmination of a panty raid or maybe one of the Priorities.

A student, Powhatan Robertson, could not get the memories of William and Mary out of his mind. He wrote on July 4, 1816: "I could not shut the door of my room for the last time without a sigh of regret...A window to the South opened into a row of most elegant elm trees whose shade & beauty always called forth the most pleasurable ideas. On the east it opened to the College yard, a more beautiful view it could not well present."

This volume, in commemoration of the three hundredth anniversary of the granting of the Royal Charter by King William III and Queen Mary II of Great Britain on February 8, 1693, contains traditions, myths and memories. The first section with its selected traditions and myths is blended with modern-day photographs of the campus; the memories in the second section are accompanied by photographs of specific decades, offering an opportunity for you to sit back and let your mind wander and to share those days as a student when life was simpler and kinder. Through added recollections of classmates, friends and fellow alumni, William and Mary will be remembered and, it is hoped, your own memories will flood back.

And, "Dear College, old in years and fame and richly old in honors, too. Time shall not dull the shining name whose gleam our songs will e'er renew. And as years go by, dear William and Mary, thy fame will never cease, but each new year rejoice to see thy children's praise to thee increase."—WILFORD KALE '66

Traditions, Myths

Twenty-Five Have Served

Twenty-five presidents and at least six acting presidents have served in the College's 300 years. While the Reverend James Blair served for fifty years, Dr. William Wilmer served the shortest term—only seven months. Three other presidents were in office thirty or more years: Bishop James Madison, Benjamin Stoddert Ewell and Lyon G. Tyler. Twelve presidents have been members of the clergy, including the first nine, while others have been educators, businessmen, lawyers and military men.

Only four times in the history of the College have there been four living presidents—including those at left: Davis Y. Paschall (1960-1971), Thomas A. Graves, Jr. (1971-1985), Paul R. Verkuil (1985-1992), and Timothy J. Sullivan (1992-).

The First President

The Reverend James Blair, William and Mary's legendary first president, holds the record for service—fifty years from 1693 to 1743. It was Blair's determination, forcefulness and arrogance that drove the fledgling College and his iron will that helped forge its destiny. Students even barred him from the main building in a 1702 Christmas prank, which he saw as a move by his enemies to threaten his power. As Commissary of the Bishop of London in Virginia, Blair was also the head of the colony's clergy and exercised an inordinate amount of power, successfully challenging and ousting three royal governors—Sir Edmund Andros, Francis Nicholson and Alexander Spotswood.

& His Wife

Sara Harrison Blair, wife of William and Mary's first president, was the College's —and probably Virginia's—first feminist. Biographers say that when she wed Blair in 1687 she refused to say the word "obey" in the marriage vows. Instead she said, "No obey." The minister refused to continue and repeated the vow, and again she said, "No obey." After a third "no obey" the ceremony continued and the marriage was pronounced.

Of Coming "Home"

One of the largest of all American college and university reunions takes place annually at the College's fall Homecoming weekend. First initiated in 1926, the program included its first parade in 1929, an activity that has survived to this day. Thousands of alumni return now for the four-day program that includes more than fifty separate activities sponsored or coordinated by the Society of the Alumni. In addition to class reunions, there are organizational reunions, sporting events and, of course, the football game. Every aspect of Homecoming is designed to continue to bind together alumni and others who have been touched by this historic College.

& Walking Together

The Homecoming Parade has weathered rain storms and the social unrest of the 1960s, and after nearly sixty-five years has survived through eras when school spirit has taken on different modes. Begun in 1929, it gathers together a wide variety of participants from within the College community. Cancelled only twice, it was postponed one day in 1976. It was for years perhaps the only parade in America seen twice, as it went up and down historic Duke of Gloucester Street.

CARROT
THE
"THYME"
your Life!
'89

The First Prize

The small medal of F.H.C., founded in 1750 as probably the first secret student society and first collegiate fraternity in America, was the first medallic prize or award presented for distinctive achievement. The most recent is the Olde Guarde medallion given to alumni upon their fiftieth class reunion. Governor Botetourt established two gold medals, first awarded in 1772 to the best scholars in classics and philosophy. The medal is still given today to the senior with the highest academic average. The Alumni Medallion for service and loyalty, with its distinctive view of the Wren Building, has been awarded by the Society of the Alumni since 1934. Other medals also are given by the law and business schools to national figures for significant accomplishments.

& The First Fraternity

Phi Beta Kappa, America's most distinguished academic honorary, was founded by students at the College of William and Mary—John Heath, Thomas Smith, Richard Booker, Armistead Smith and John Jones— in the Apollo Hall of the Raleigh Tavern on December 5, 1776. In the ritual the founders named friendship, morality and literature as their guiding precepts.

1693 · THE OLDE GUARDE · 1975 · THEIR MAJESTIES' ROYALL COLLEDGE IN VIRGINIA

Green Vistas

The College during Thomas Jefferson's time (1760-1762) was surrounded by forests and glens. There were few encroachments; man and nature lived in harmony. The author of the Declaration of Independence felt "the College" should always look out upon the country and from there draw its strength. Today, westward from the Wren a green vista moves through the heart of the campus, beginning at the Sunken Garden and Crim Dell and moving toward Lake Matoaka. From the boxwood hedges and crape myrtle to azaleas and magnolia and into the forests of oak and pine, today's Jefferson Prospect maintains a natural and philosophical connection with the past.

& A Lively Legend

A living memorial to John W. H. Crim '01, the dell west of the Sunken Garden, with flowering shrubs of azaleas, camellia and mountain laurel, is a favorite campus spot for a leisurely stroll, quiet meditation, romance, and folklore: if a young woman walks alone across the Chinese-style bridge over the pond, she's forever doomed to spinsterhood; if she walks across with a young man and stops to dally halfway and kisses him, she is destined to marry him. That will not happen if she changes her mind, crosses the bridge again, and throws the poor fellow into the water.

Of Women

Women were not allowed to attend the College for its first 225 years. They were admitted in 1918, not as a move toward equal status and opportunity, but rather because World War I had brought a sudden decline in enrollment and the College was in desperate need of more students to maintain its financial health. Women gradually became accepted, participating in clubs and organizations and in their own intercollegiate athletic teams, but it was not until 1969 that a woman—Nancy Terrill—was elected president of the student body.

& A Legacy of Perfection

In the annals of the W&M Theatre, the name Althea Hunt is legendary. Miss Hunt's drive for perfection molded the "educational theatre" in its formative decades. Her disciplinary efforts crafted actors and actresses steeped in all elements of the theatre—from the stage to the workshop and from the box office to the lighting booth. Among former W&M students to gain Broadway and Hollywood acclaim are Linda Lavin '59 and Glenn Close '74.

Ambassadors of Song

Over the past half century, William and Mary Choir members have been the best-known ambassadors of the College. Although there was a choral ensemble for many years, including a male glee club at the turn of the century, the tradition of today's choir was developed through the directorial efforts of Dr. Carl A. "Pappy" Fehr and Dr. Frank T. Lendrim. The hallmark of a Fehr-trained choir (from 1945 to 1974) was its musical versatility and staging, state tours and nationwide Christmas television programs. Since 1974 Dr. Lendrim's choirs have distinguished themselves through a varied repertoire, European tours and creation of a smaller group, the Botetourt Chamber Singers.

& Good Will

A Christmas television program taped on campus in the early 1970s by the William and Mary Choir created such an impression and good will that it was still being shown by several West Coast television stations more than a dozen years later. Today, choir members on their European tours always reflect on the College, whether it be chatting with Princess Margriet of the Netherlands on the steps of Het Loo Palace; serenading the American ambassador at dinner in the armor-lined hall at Hatfield House in England; or bringing their voices in song to Westminster Abbey in London.

Of Three Queens

There is a feeling of majesty with the appearance of the regally red- and black-clad Queen's Guard in their tall English-style busbees. This guard of honor was established in 1961 as a student organization in uniforms styled of the English tradition. With its motto, "Victory shall come to the Worthy," the Guard pays tribute to three English queens: Mary, who helped found the College in 1693; Anne, who came to the school's financial aid after the College burned in 1705; and Elizabeth II, the reigning British monarch who visited the College in 1957, strengthening nearly three centuries of the strong ties between the school and the English crown.

& "The Best of Men"

For nearly 150 years, the statue of Norborne Berkeley, Baron de Botetourt, guarded the front of the Wren Building; it now stands in Swem Library. Although the royal governor served less than two years, Lord Botetourt was a member of the College's Board of Visitors, serving one year as rector, and was a favorite of students, attending chapel services with them each morning. When he died in 1770, Virginians proclaimed him "the best of governors and the best of men," buried him in a vault beneath the Wren Chapel, and commissioned a statue in his honor.

"A Pious Education"

The Sir Christopher Wren Building was "The College" for nearly a century. An early professor, Hugh Jones, wrote in 1724 that the structure was "first modelled by [Wren], adapted to the Nature of the Country by the Gentlemen there." In its hallowed halls, students and professors lived and studied and legislators, on two occasions, conducted the affairs of the colony. Today, it stands as a living monument—the oldest academic building still in use in America—to the vision 300 years ago of Virginians who sought "a certain Place of universal study" so that the Youth of the Colony "may be piously educated in good Letters and Manners."

& Fraternity Pranks

Beneath the floor of the chapel in the Wren Building are a number of crypts similar to many other Anglican churches of the period. It is not known exactly how many persons have been buried there, but the two best known are Peyton Randolph, the first president of the Continental Congress, who lived most of his life in Williamsburg, and Lord Botetourt, royal governor and a friend of the College. Fraternity pranksters reportedly opened the crypts in the late 1960s and scattered what little remained.

A Long Rivalry

The first organized intercollegiate athletic team to represent the College was in football, organized in 1893. The team lost its first game with another college in 1894 to Hampden-Sydney, 24-0. W&M's longest rivalry on the gridiron began in 1898 with the University of Richmond and now is the oldest in the South and the fourth oldest in the nation. Baseball began in 1895 and track was started in 1917, but the first scheduled meet with Virginia Military Institute was cancelled when war was declared.

Women's sports began in 1918 with intramural basketball, and field hockey was started the next year. In 1920 intercollegiate women's competition began with basketball, tennis and track.

& Mr. Cary's Field

Mr. Cary's Field—where athletic events have been held for nearly a century—was literally the land owned by the Cary family and donated to the College during the presidency of Lyon G. Tyler. Two Cary ancestors were associated with the College: Archibald was a student in 1740, and Henry is believed to have built the Brafferton in 1723 and the President's House nine years later.

"The Goose Hangs High"

The William and Mary Theatre was established by Professor Althea Hunt, whose first student performance—"The Goose Hangs High"—was staged on December 18, 1926, formally opening old Phi Beta Kappa Hall as a theater.

Professor Howard Scammon '34 continued Miss Hunt's theatrical legacy. With the able assistance of Albert Haak's master stage-craftsmanship and Roger Sherman's inventive lighting and staging, Scammon's theatre set an enviable reputation for collegiate educational productions. Professors Louis Catron and Richard Palmer are among today's theatre cadre whose dedication and demands for excellence continue William and Mary's theatre tradition.

& "A Pastoral Colloquy"

The earliest known student performance at the College —"A Pastoral Colloquy"—was presented in Latin and performed for the royal governor in 1702. The first theatre in America opened in Williamsburg in 1716, and some plays later were known to be presented by students from the College. *The Virginia Gazette* reported in its September 3-10 issue in 1736 that: "This evening will be performed at the Theatre, by the Young Gentlemen of the College, the Tragedy of Cato."

The Good Sciences

As a college of the "good Arts and Sciences," William and Mary frequently is remembered more as a school of arts and letters than of science. Even from the early days of the College, scientific apparatus was secured to conduct experiments and illustrate exercises. Probably one of the most outstanding of the early professors of natural philosophy was Dr. William Small, whose lasting contribution was the innovation of the modern lecture system about 1758. Thomas Jefferson, a student at the College from 1760 to 1762, said "it was my great good fortune" to have Dr. Small as a professor, "a man profound in most of the useful branches of science" who "fixed the destinies of my life." William Barton Rogers, an eminent professor a half century later, left W&M and later founded the Massachusetts Institute of Technology.

& A Vision

With vision and determination, William and Mary scientist and teacher Dr. Donald Davis fought the academic and political battles in the 1930s to secure the creation of a department of marine science that later became the Virginia Institute of Marine Science. Located at Gloucester Point, the Institute today with its graduate programs and extensive research plays a leading role in estuarine research and is a key scientific component in the multistate effort to clean up the Chesapeake Bay and its tributaries.

All Souls College

The stained glass window of Sir Christopher Wren in the lobby of the Marshall-Wythe School of Law is one of two windows—the other of William Blackstone, the great English legal scholar—given to the College in 1980 by All Souls College, Oxford University. These windows were removed from Oxford during the bombing in World War II and never replaced.

Wren is believed to have been involved, either personally or through his royal post of surveyor-general, in the design or "modelling" of the main College building of 1695.

& The College of Arms

"Vert a Colledge, or Edifice Mason'd Argent in Chief a Sun rising Or the Hemisphere proper" or "buildings in silver on a green field with a blue sky above containing part of a golden sun" was the description by the College of Arms in London of the original William & Mary coat of arms given May 14, 1694. The arms was part of the College's official seal until about 1783 when the "Temple Seal" with its Greek-style building was first used. The original arms was lost until 1926 when the imprint of that original seal was discovered on a 1749 document.

WREN

Shared Dreams

Matoaka is the Indian name for Pocahontas, whose father Powhatan was principal chief when the English settlers landed in 1607 at Jamestown. The lake has been, in some way, part of the College lands since the beginning. It was around its shores that Indians wore paths into the soil and the young Jefferson, Marshall, the Randolphs and their contemporaries walked, mused and dreamed their dreams. Later, as the core of the College Woods, it became a park with hiking and horseback trails and canoeing. Now it has been designated by the College and the city of Williamsburg as a major conservancy area.

& A Common Glory

"The Common Glory," an outdoor drama that told the story of the founding fathers and the beginning of the nation, was first performed on the shore of Lake Matoaka in 1947. Staged nightly during the summer months in a large amphitheatre, the production utilized many William and Mary faculty and staff and featured many students as actors and choir members. The performances ended in 1976.

Pomp, Circumstance

Believed to be one of the most distinctive maces in academic America, the College Mace was given by alumni and students in 1923 at the College's 230th anniversary. There are eleven sections: an eagle; a sphere, symbolizing unity; the College arms; the arms of the Chancellors; the seven seals of colonial Virginia; the F.H.C., Phi Beta Kappa and Lord Botetourt medals; names of twenty-eight noted alumni; the Earth, which symbolizes the College's worldwide influence; colonial governors; forty-two distinguished men in Virginia history prior to the Revolution; and the names of W&M's presidents.

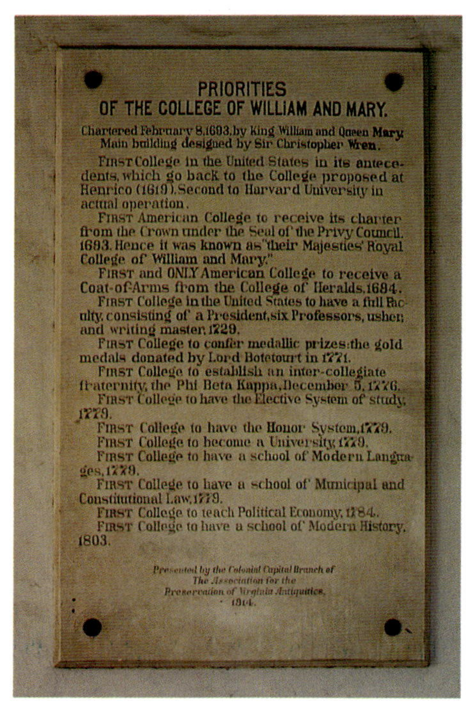

& A List of Firsts

Following the return of students in 1888 to the College, President Lyon G. Tyler confronted the task of rebuilding the school's reputation. He developed the unique scheme of "Priorities" denoting William and Mary's distinctive place in higher education. Into marble and history were chiseled thirteen FIRSTS—Tyler's way of creating an instant credibility for the 200-year-old institution. Some FIRSTS, however, now pose questions for historians: Is the date of origin of the Honor System correct? Was there really a school of medicine? Is William and Mary the only college to receive a coat of arms? Wasn't a professorship in the fine arts in 1779 the first in the country?

Of White Jackets

White jackets at the College, especially at Homecoming, signify membership in the Order of the White Jacket, established in 1972 to recognize and honor those students who worked their way through school waiting tables in the dining hall or later working in food service at the College or Colonial Williamsburg. Its roster includes a governor, a college president, doctors, lawyers, bankers, prominent business executives, ministers and civic leaders. This unusual "fraternity" of kindred spirits stresses the fact that it was in their college days when they discovered the essence of leadership in the service to others.

& Dining Halls

Students during the Colonial days took their room and board as well as their classes in "The College," now called the Wren Building. The dining room was the Great Hall. In the late 19th century, there was a dining room in a building adjacent to old Taliaferro Hall on Jamestown Road. Trinkle Hall was built in 1926, and its little cafe became popular for smaller groups. When the Campus Center was built, its Wigwam became a fast-order student hangout. Now it's known as The Marketplace.

Of Holiday Tradition

The Yule Log dates from medieval times and burned throughout the twelve days of Christmas. The tradition was brought to America with the first English settlers. It became a part of the College holiday scene in 1930 when Dr. Grace Warren Landrum, dean of women, introduced the custom with elaborate costumes. Students brought the log into the Great Hall and the youngest child present poured wine over the log and tossed the first piece of holly on the fire for good luck. Everyone then tossed sprigs of holly onto the fire, reviving the superstition that cares of the past year go up in flames with the holly.

& Frivolity

College President John Stewart Bryan, dressed as a royal governor with a double-bottom wig, presided as the Lord of the Manor at the costume Christmas party planned for faculty and students. Staged in old Phi Beta Kappa Hall, the program featured food, dancing and entertainment with elaborate decorations. Faculty members dressed in Colonial costumes, while students wore costumes of their choice. Sororities and fraternities also performed skits. In recent years the College president has dressed as Santa Claus and read the traditional "Night Before Christmas."

The Colonial Campus

After several Indian youths had studied at The Brafferton, the College's Indian School, one chief lamented, "When they came back to us, they were bad runners, ignorant of every means of living in the wood, unable to bear either cold or hunger ... were therefore neither fit for hunters, warriors, or councilors; they were totally good for nothing." Nevertheless, the school was maintained in some fashion for sixty years or more during the 18th century, and a number of Indians attended. The Brafferton, which was built in 1723 with funds from the estate of the English scientist and philosopher Sir Robert Boyle, the President's House, and the Wren Building are the three remaining original structures from the colonial campus.

& The Revolution

The President's House was built in 1732. Each of the school's twenty-five presidents has used the home. It was damaged during the American Revolution, and French King Louis XVI contributed funds to its restoration. Considered one of the best examples of Georgian architecture in the U. S., it now contains a collection of antiques befitting its age and status within the college community.

A Sunken Garden

A bit of old England was envisioned in 1935 when the Sunken Garden was fashioned from the field behind the Wren. Reminiscent of the grounds of London's Chelsea Hospital, the Garden is surrounded by a tall boxwood hedge with scattered crape myrtle trees. Through the years it has been the scene of formal dances, ROTC drills, classes, Frisbee tosses, touch football and even a little romance. During the Revolutionary War, Patrick Henry selected the site as a place for the encampment of militia destined to join Washington's army in the North and it later served as a bivouac area for many soldiers preparing to fight the British at nearby Yorktown.

& A Gala Setting

A canopy of stars over the Sunken Garden added to a gala setting for the Finals dances from 1937 to 1940. With elaborate decorations, Hal Kemp, Glenn Miller, Gene Krupa and Woody Herman were among the famous dance bands to play. The outdoor dance was revived in 1963 and 1964 with the Maynard Ferguson and Zi Zentner orchestras. In addition to the annual Homecoming Dance, weekend dances also were held.

"A Link Among the Days . . ."

The Society of the Alumni, founded July 4, 1842, at the suggestion of College President Thomas Roderick Dew, provides "a link among the days to knit the generations each with each." The nation's sixth oldest alumni organization, the Society had about 500 alumni at its founding and now boasts more than 75,000 men and women on its rolls. For its first eighty years, the Society functioned little beyond providing a prominent speaker for the annual Alumni Day program. With the support of College President Dr. J.A.C. Chandler, the Society was incorporated in 1923, began Homecoming activities in the 1920s and finally moved into its own facilities—Alumni House—in 1971. From chapter meetings and sponsored foreign trips to Alumni College with its academic thrust and Homecoming with its dances and parties, the Society endeavors to give alumni opportunities to maintain ties with fellow classmates as well as their alma mater.

Mary Land Gill '28
Alumni Medallion Recipient

"Graduates will go forth . . ."

In the early years of the College, each student completing his schooling delivered an oration in Latin at graduation exercises, the first of which was held in the Wren Building in 1700. For many years in the 19th century, graduation was held on the Fourth of July, always with a certain degree of pomp and ceremony. For decades this century, the year-ending convocations were held in the front yard of the Wren, but in 1976 were transferred indoors to William and Mary Hall. Beginning in 1978 in a desire to retain a link between the old and the new, students gather the night before graduation at the Wren for a candlelight service, and today the walk across campus also begins at the Wren just minutes before graduation begins.

& The Bell Tolls On

From 1888 until his death in 1955, Henry Billups daily rang the bell in the cupola of the Wren Building to mark the beginning of classes. In recent years, to mark the last day of classes, each senior who wishes to do so may ring that same bell that has tolled since 1859. All day long the sound of the bell echoes through the campus, celebrating the completion of undergraduate days and recalling the times when President Benjamin S. Ewell rang the bell during the silent years to keep the College's Royal Charter alive.

& Memories

And I knew then that these faces, these lives, would never all be united again.

I remember standing at the top of the Wren Building stairs on a warm evening in May of 1984, looking out over a large crowd of friends and classmates. I could see the lights of DOG Street twinkling in the distance. It was a special night and my heart was full of pride and memories of the time I had spent with the classmates in front of me. As the vice president of the senior class, I stood before the graduating students, the only woman to speak at the Candlelight ceremony that night. I was the final speaker and I provided one last glimpse of the campus, the images that had filled our daily lives: ringing the bell in the Wren Building, strolling over the Crim Dell, checking at the Sundial for a big sister clue. I was so proud and so grateful for all that had been accomplished and all that had been given. We are enriched not only by what we gather, but also by what we give away. As I finished, I lit the first candle and watched the glow spread across 1,000 hands to illuminate the faces before me. And I knew then that these faces, these lives, would never all be united again, except in the memories of this ancient place. I stood and watched as the crowd turned and the candles flickered and died as they spread through the darkness like the tail of a meteor shining softly in a quiet summer's sky.

JOANNA ASHWORTH '84

It was the age of the flapper, "Oxford bags," raccoon coats, peekaboo hats, saddle shoes, tea dances and knickers.

One September afternoon, in the mid-1920s, a young man got off the train at the Williamsburg train depot and walked up to the town. He was a British Subject, but as the story goes, by the time that he reached the College Corner, he was a Southerner and a Democrat.

Certainly as he stood at the College Gate and looked at the three mellow brick buildings shaded by tall trees, it was just like he had hoped it would be.

Of the three early eighteenth-century buildings, it was obvious that the one on the right with the porch across its front was a residence and so must be the President's House. The smaller building on his left had, as he had read, been intended as a school for the Indians, but as the tribesmen showed no interest in an academic education, the charming building had served through the years as everything from a dormitory to a Faculty Club.

Strolling happily down the center brick walk, he introduced himself to Lord Botetourt, the statue of the Colonial Governor of Virginia who had stood in the exact center of the College Yard for about two centuries.

Still happy, he walked through the stately, though shabby, Wren Building to its rear arcade. There he stopped in dismay. Before him stood several barracks which, he was to learn, had been given to the College after World War II by a nearby army camp which was closing down.

What on earth were they doing here? A sign on one of them explained it was the chemistry building!

Was that where he was to teach? In that shack? For a moment he began to wonder about the schedules of outbound trains…

Just then the door marked "Chemistry Department" opened and out came two laughing gentlemen. Both were dressed in immaculate white and each man carried in his hand … a tennis racquet! Being an avid tennis player, that did it!

Never again during the pleasant, rewarding years that followed, did Dr. William G. Guy (the man who was to be-

come the head of the chemistry department, and my husband) ever give a thought to leaving the College of William and Mary.

Little could he ever realize the great influence and inspiration that he would be for generations of chemistry students and that someday a modern chemistry building would have a lecture hall named in his honor.

GLADYS BENNETT GUY '24

Memories which surround our college days do indeed constitute "the link among the days which bind the generations each to each." How can one separate them or place one above another?

I hark back to late-night strolls across the ancient campus when Lord Botetourt seemed to come alive and the spirits of Jefferson, Marshall, Ewell and countless others passed by, talking of events long gone. Washington and others strolled Duke of Gloucester.

Memories of "bull sessions" in dormitories and fraternity houses compete for attention. One is reminded of time spent waiting on tables in the dining halls among rambunctious freshmen or coeds turning up pretty noses at the current bill-o-fare.

One thinks, too, of friendships formed that endured through the decades. Unforgettable are track meets

20

It was the age of the flapper, "Oxford bags," raccoon coats, peekaboo hats, saddle shoes, tea dances, bow ties and knickers. The 1920s saw the first talking movies; a visit to the U.S. by the Prince of Wales; the St. Valentine's Day massacre; Republicans in the White House; Charles A. Lindbergh a hero; and Billy Mitchell at a court-martial.

In Williamsburg, it was before the Rockefeller restoration. There was a grass plot down the middle of Duke of Gloucester Street. Mr. Casey's store, the Norfolk Cafe and the Candy Kitchen, the Pocahontas Tea Room, the Imperial Theater, Owens Garage, the College Shop, and Mrs. Binn's Shop were busy "uptown" near the College. "Downtown" near the Powder Horn there were the Greek Revival Baptist Church, Peninsula Garage and Williamsburg Motor Company, First National Bank, Peninsula Bank, the post office and the Colonial Hotel.

At William and Mary, Dr. Chandler was president and Miss Pearl Jones was his new secretary. Women students were still new to the campus, and Jefferson Hall was built for them with a small gymnasium and the "bathtub" swimming pool. Miss Bessie Porter Taylor was social director while Kremer J. Hoke was dean of the College and William T. Hodges served as dean of freshmen.

Students finally became involved in the Honor System governance. Social rules were strict: definite boundaries were set for women students, who couldn't walk on the "men's side" of campus except to go to the library. The first block of Duke of Gloucester Street was the town boundary for coeds.

Campus expansion boomed with the construction of Jefferson, Barrett, Old Dominion, Monroe, old Rogers, old Phi Beta Kappa, Blow Gym and Washington Hall. Science and Citizenship and Ewell Dorm were near the Wren.

The law school was revived in 1922, and in 1923 the Society of the Alumni became incorporated. The Megaphone Club was organized for cheerleaders. Homecoming and the William and Mary Theatre began in 1926; May Day was a big event. The Cotillion and German clubs sponsored major dances, and sometimes the Indian Serenaders played.

Two of the Wise Men remained on the faculty for part of the decade: Drs. Van Franklin Garrett and John Lesslie Hall. There were Coaches Driver, Gooch and Barksdale; favorites, "Doc" Billups, Drs. Pollard and Swem. There were scores of clubs like the Walking Sticks, Southside, Northern Lights, Waiter's Club and the Philomathean, Whitehall, J. Lesslie Hall and Phoenix literary societies. Presidents Harding and Coolidge came to campus to receive honorary degrees, and the Marshall-Wythe School of Government and Citizenship was created.

with old rivals. For example, there is the time I missed part of the installation of my local fraternity into Phi Kappa Tau during a cross-country race with the University of Richmond, out-running every opponent save one and still not scoring because too many teammates were better.

The thoughts turn to Saturday night dances in the gymnasium of Jefferson Hall, with music by a college group, or the weekend formals in Blow Gym with imported orchestras.

One recalls the pleasures of holding pretty girls and whirling around the floor when at any other time it was close to "shipping offense" to hold hands without dreaming of a goodnight kiss or keeping a date out beyond the 10 or 11 o'clock deadline.

Then, there were the pep rallies out near old Cary Field with huge bonfires on the eve of games with rival colleges. Also there was the annual special train by the C&O from Williamsburg to Richmond for the Thanksgiving Day game, winning four straight years.

Most of all, to be fair about it, one must give thanks for the magnificent faculty assembled by President Julian Alvin Carroll Chandler who took over from Lyon G. Tyler in the wake of World War I and served until his death in 1934.

Chandler, who brought William and Mary into the twentieth century, nagged the General Assembly into providing scarce funds and starting a new campus.

The names of that faculty roll by, one by one — men, and a few women, who demonstrated matchless loyalty despite low salaries and difficult living conditions.

There was John Garland Pollard, former attorney general of Virginia, destined to succeed Harry F. Byrd as governor. He made Virginia government a vibrant subject for all freshmen. There was Richard L. Morton, whose class in Virginia history was a must. A copious note-taker, he produced a series of volumes on the era from Jamestown to the Revolution. I loved the man. Beyond classes we were the tenor section of the tiny Presbyterian Church on Palace Green. Long after his retirement, I urged him to complete his history but he was tired. He even offered to give me his notes through the Civil War if I would finish the job, something I had to decline.

Another favorite was Dr. Earl G. Swem, a remarkable man who took over a tiny library, living to see it greatly expanded and eventually a large new structure built and named for himself. His handiwork is seen in hundreds of historical markers along Virginia's highways.

I shall never forget his gratitude when, as a member of the Board of Visitors, I assured him the library ranked first with me alongside a student union. Having my name on a plaque in that library is a distinct honor.

Best remembered is youthful Havilah Babcock, native of Appomattox, who taught journalism, short stories and English. He was my mentor, and above all, my adviser as editor of *The Flat Hat.* I often went on trips with him to Richmond and to other extension classes. We were close friends and I visited in his home, enjoying his company and that of his cheerful wife.

The name Havilah was imposed on him by a father who took delight in obscure Old Testament names. This caused him to name his only son "Huckleberry" or just plain "Huck," with assurance that Huck could select his own name when he felt like doing so.

Havilah moved to the University of South Carolina as professor of English, a real loss to William and Mary. Near the end of World War II, traveling on orders, I paused at his home in Columbia where he was dying of cancer. I asked him what name Huck chose.

"Guess," he replied with an impish grin.

"Don't tell me," I exclaimed.

"Yep," he said, "Havilah, Jr."

Almost all of that faculty are long gone, but they linger fondly in my memory. I could write a book, but I'd better not — it would be endless.

M. CARL ANDREWS '27

Can you imagine having to check into your dormitory every night on a chart taped to the walls at the end or the middle of every floor in each of the women's dorms?

Proctors checked the charts after the 10 p.m. bell rang curfew and all outside doors were locked. If you were late, you were "campused" for a month.

Also, at 11 p.m. all lights were out. If you wanted to study, you used a flashlight. This was never questioned in 1926.

Can you imagine anyone's applying for admission to the College in August and being accepted for September opening? That's what happened to me in 1926.

My father jumped on a train for Williamsburg and upon arrival at the College (without an appointment), he asked to see Dr. J.A.C. Chandler. Dr. Chandler saw him and listened to his plea. Dr. Chandler's reply was, "I don't have a vacancy of any kind, but you send that girl down here anyway. I'll find a place for her." And he did — in a private home on Boundary Street.

That's how I entered the College.

Can you imagine having to go to compulsory chapel services once a week on an assigned day before you went to your first morning class? As you entered chapel, you dropped a slip of paper with your name on it into a box placed at the door for that purpose. These were checked, and your cuts appeared on your report card. You were allowed cuts only for certain valid reasons.

This was never questioned in 1926.

ELIZABETH W. LANIER '30

The night watchman caught Bill kissing one of the girls in the sorority house. The watchman (Al) asked if he wanted to turn himself in or if he should. Bill said, "I will." So the next morning he went to see Miss Bessie Taylor and explained his case. She said with a slight smile on her face, "Well, just don't let it happen again."

Bill had been working getting ads for *The Flat Hat* before the Final Dance. His roommate had to work and asked Bill to take his date to the dance. Bill rented a tuxedo, took his shower and fell across the bed. Next thing he knew, it was morning. Fortunately, one of the other boys noticed Sue Pollard (Bill's date) was not at the dance, went over to her house at intermission and took her to the dance. Bill said the worst thing he had to do was go over and apologize to Miss Pollard. He said she was most gracious.

Bill won the William and Mary Medallion and they had to wake him up to tell him!

WILLIAM G. THOMPSON, JR. '27

It was the time between the wars, and Williamsburg and the College struggled with the Great Depression.

Saying good-bye to my parents at the edge of campus and knowing even through my tears that it was the beginning of four fabulous years ... the incredible deflation of receiving a *D* on my first freshman theme ... feeling persecuted at having to eat in the freshmen girls' dining room until we realized how much we liked having those cute waiters all to ourselves ... President Roosevelt's speech and John Stewart Bryan's inauguration as President of the College ... the dreaded Sophomore Tribunal and being required to walk past the statue of Lord Botetourt and tip our "duc" caps ... carrying laundry to the sisters at the house as part of our pledge duty ... the College Shop and getting a "tin roof" sundae for ten cents ... "break" dances and hoping you wouldn't get stuck ... being mentioned in the "dirt" column of *The Flat Hat* ... walking through the campus blanketed with snow to carol in Sorority Court ... going back to campus after Christmas to face term papers and exams ... old Phi Beta Kappa Hall as the setting for Douglas Southall Freeman's lectures, for President Bryan's Christmas parties, for Women's Student Government meetings where we settled what we considered momentous problems, for those wonderful productions by Miss Althea Hunt starring our own May Fielder and Carl Buffington ... working on play sets under Mr. Leslie Cheek's direction ... Dr. Jackson greeting latecomers to English class with "Good morning, did you sleep well?" ... correcting freshmen English themes and entertaining the sisters with their "goofs" ... riding in a rumble seat to Richmond to shop ... weeklong rain and ankle-deep mud on Duke of Gloucester Street ... working frantically on our float for Homecoming parade and then seeing it go soggy in the rain ... spring and Williamsburg, a fairyland of daffodils, hyacinths and forsythia ... May Day in the Sunken Garden ... mobs of tourists on campus during Garden Week and someone asking the location of the "Bird" Building ... Hal Kemp's Band at Final dances in the Sunken Garden on perfect June evenings ... graduation under the trees in front of the Wren Building and feeling torn between reluctance to leave and anticipation of the future.

JANE SPEAKMAN HAUGE '38

Numerous students exchanged wedding vows in historic Bruton Parish Church but it wasn't until 1935 that the first William and Mary couple was married in the Wren Chapel. Despite popular belief that College President John Edwin Pomfret's wedding was the first held there, it was actually another William and Mary couple who started this tradition. The day following their graduation, Margaret Mary "Midge" Parmelee and F. Barrett Horton were married in the chapel on June 11, 1935, at 11 a.m. It was a beautiful ceremony followed by a wedding breakfast in the garden of the Travis House in Colonial Williamsburg.

The Hortons' trip to the altar had quite a bumpy start. In order to be married in the chapel, the couple went through reels of red tape and had to petition both President Bryan and his assistant, Charlie Duke. Both officials were concerned that a "precedent" would be set and other couples would want to be married there. After much debate, they finally relented. Complications continued, however; even the priest had to obtain a special permit to conduct the ceremony.

The Hortons enjoyed 40 years together before his death in 1975. And they indeed set a precedent! Over the years, thousands of alumni have begun their married lives within the beautiful setting of the Wren Chapel.

AS TOLD BY MARGARET MARY PARMELEE SHERIDAN '35

My first encounter, that I recall, with Dr. Harold Fowler, was the start of a love/hate relationship which had a happy ending. Coming from a small town and a small high school, the College lecture classes were a total surprise (and probably a shock) to me. It was my freshman year in which I soon learned about the fun of "bull sessions" and staying up late. Sleepy, and not paying proper attention in Dr. Fowler's morning history lecture, I yawned several times. Suddenly, I heard my name, "Miss Grodecoeur, if you are bored, you may leave this classroom." I muttered something to the effect that I was not bored, just tired, and remained in my seat.

Thereafter, I paid attention, studied my history, sweated over the blue-book exam (another abrupt change from high school) and, thereafter, took as many Harold Fowler courses as I could, "fell in love" with him (as a teacher and person), and will never forget the night he "cut in" to dance with me at a Saturday night hop. He was an inspiration; someone I will never forget. Those were years of fulfillment and growth which enriched my life then and now.

FRANCES L. GRODECOEUR '39

At age 16, in September 1939, I came to W&M by train to begin my freshman year. I had never been to Williamsburg, but was excited at having been accepted at such a fine, historic college. I had been told the W&M campus was one of the most beautiful in the country.

When I got off the train at the Chesapeake & Ohio station, a few other freshmen and I were offered rides to our dormitories by upperclassmen with cars. I hopped into a convertible with my luggage and told them my dorm was Old Dominion Hall. They drove me and another freshman to the "beautiful campus" of Eastern State Hospital (then located on South Henry Street, on the site of the present law school). They pointed to an old run-down stone building three stories high, with bars on all its windows. They said Room 327 was on the third floor, then drove off, leaving us to trudge about fifty yards to the door.

I couldn't believe the campus looked so run-down. When we got to the door, we rang a bell, as the door was locked. An attendant in a white uniform came

30

It was still the time between the wars, and Williamsburg and the College struggled with the Great Depression. The 1930s were the heyday of radio; the end to Prohibition; the Great Drought and then dust. FDR became president with his New Deal and its NRA, CCC, WPA, and PWA. The glamour girl was created, and late in the decade Hollywood films blossomed with "The Wizard of Oz," and "Gone with the Wind."

In Williamsburg Mr. Rockefeller restored the colonial grandeur to the Wren, Brafferton and President's House as well as a third of the town. As the historic area took shape, businesses were moved nearer the College except for the A&P and Penders and Rexall No. 2, which remained "downtown." In the new business area Angelo Costas operated the Capitol Restaurant, known later as the "Middle Greeks;" the new Imperial Theatre and the West End Market opened across from each other; the Williamsburg Restaurant quickly became the "Corner Greeks" and joined Douglas' Bakery, Frazier-Callis and Colonial Barbershop. Churches—Methodist, Baptist and Presbyterian—moved across from the College, and segregation was still a way of life.

At William and Mary Dr. Chandler died and was succeeded by Mr. Bryan and a new College era. President Franklin D. Roosevelt visited campus. A flight school flourished with Col. Popp and Y. O. Kent as instructors. The Sunken Garden was dug and planted and the stadium at Cary Field opened. Student governance was still divided for men and women. The Alumni Medallion was first given and the Alumni Gazette *began publication. Finals were held in the garden and Mr. Bryan began his Christmas parties. Dean Landrum initiated the Yule Log ceremony.*

Faculty and staff favorites included Herbert Bridges, Dr. R. G. Robb, Dr. R. C. Young, Dr. Donald Davis, Dr. Richard Morton, Dr. J. R. Geiger, Miss Emily Calkins and Coaches Kellison, Scrap Chandler, Tucker Jones, Miss Barksdale and Miss Wynne-Roberts. Fraternities and sororities continued to flourish as did the debate clubs, glee clubs and band.

The Colonial Echo *began its fourth decade and* The Flat Hat *its third. When the winters were hard, ice-skating was possible on Matoaka with its Holly Point Cabin. The* Royalist *was born as were the department of fine arts, the Clayton-Grimes Biology Club and the Backdrop Club. And the beaches of the York and James were popular. A pony, Wampo, first appeared as a football mascot.*

to the door. He looked at us and laughed: "Welcome to the beautiful College of William and Mary." I looked dumb-founded! He finally relented, and told us this was "the nut house!" He called us a taxi, which took us to O.D. The cabbie said he had been hauling freshmen from Eastern State after each train had arrived and were met by our "Big Brothers."

IRA B. DWORKIN '43, '48 B.C.L.

Pre-World War II students at the College were most fortunate. The campus abounded with vivid administrators and professors, their presence uniting the campus. Colorful President John Stewart Bryan set the tone and pace for town and gown alike. His radiance incited and attracted the crème de la crème of academia.

Mentors for me included Dr. Earl Gregg Swem, Librarian. I was required to spend hours in "his" library. This pleasant building was sunny (though steaming hot and not air conditioned in summer). It had the air of a classic cluttered atmosphere recalling the great hall of a large English country manor. Each morning we officially opened the building together. I arrived slightly early to pick up and read the headlines of a hand-delivered *New York Times* thrown on the steps. His cheerful "Good morning, William" gave a needed spark to a long gruelling day.

I was forced to take an overload of required courses, including graduate classes, as a transfer student. Ironically, I had no time to take any classes conducted by my now-devoted friend, "National Living Treasure," Leslie Cheek, Jr. I vividly recall my first sight of Leslie from my window in Monroe 315. Impeccably groomed, he was boldly striding below. His uniquely designed Fine Arts Building (President Bryan had requested him to set up a fine arts department) gave me silent solace to steal away from Swem for a few moments to pursue art books and periodicals briefly.

Other inspiring professors were Dr. Richard Morton, history, and Dean Melville Jones, literature, and the splendid theatre productions of Miss Althea Hunt (with many stunning sets designed by Leslie). Leslie's designed and executed Sunken Garden (I dubbed it the Sunken Garden due to its poor drainage system) Dance Pavilion was nationally acclaimed.

The Class of '39 graduation ceremony was held in the Wren entrance yard, a stunning setting. A much admired literary figure, Ellen Glasgow, received an honorary degree making the occasion even more memorable. Fortunately my sister took a black and white photograph of her in academic regalia, which I treasure.

On every visit I enter Wren and somehow make it up to the Great Hall to pay my respects to the presidents past, particularly Dr. Bryan and Dr. Graves (Tom the Great).

WILLIAM D. EPPES '39

Shared memories are the golden thread that knits the generations each to each in love for our Alma Mater.

Of the some 1,100-member student body, women were in a decided minority, but, oh, how we loved that stag line!

The College operated its own farm, and served "It" in the dining hall! Remember the mashed potatoes with that "strong" gravy; carrots and peas; stewed tomatoes — all served in those large, heavy dishes, while rolls were passed "through the air."

Classes were taught on Saturdays, with only one day off, Thanksgiving, before Christmas. Ah, yes, the big bonfire and rally on Thanksgiving eve before the game with Richmond — enlivened now and then by pranksters from the University of Richmond who came late and vandalized Lord Botetourt!

And the "bull sessions," those stimulating extracurricular indulgences — often more exciting than some classes. Student pranks, yes, but not viciously contrived. And some of us do well recall that famous night watchman named "Al," who possessed the "sneaky approach."

Some of us had Dean Hoke for philosophy of education; Donald Davis for biology; Richard L. Morton for history; "Goot" Gregory for freshman English; Mel Jones for English literature; "Bill" Guy or "Doc" Robb for chemistry; W.A.R. Goodwin for "Biblical lit."; J. D. Carter for French; Walter Montgomery for Latin — and, who else? Oh, yes, Dean Grace Landrum invited the women on Sunday afternoons to her house for tea, and to hear the crickets on the hearth!

Dr. Earl Gregg Swem moved so quietly in the library that you didn't know he was there until he tapped your shoulder and whispered, " This is a library, not a matrimonial stage."

In the Treasurer's Office was a man named Vernon L. Nunn who assisted so many of us in "making it," because in 1929 came the Stock Market Crash, heralding the "Great Depression." (Some fathers had to forego smoking or tobacco chewing.) Despite the tight times, we somehow remained a happy, exciting class. In retrospect, it didn't take much to make us happy! In fact the annual swimming party at Yorktown Beach was a real highlight.

Who can forget Henry ("Doc") Billups, the Bell Ringer? He wore impressively that large gold chain across his vest, with a "railroad" watch on one end, and a little gold-looking cup on the other. He had acquired the little cup because of growing weary of returning alumni who offered him a "nip," but bemoaned that they had nothing to pour it in! He rang the bell as if he were shaking the hand of a friend. Not only for change of classes, ten minutes before the hour, and on the hour, but also fifteen minutes before the curfew, and then the final dong when doors to the women's dorms were locked.

DAVIS Y. PASCHALL '32

A hellish World War and its aftermath made their imprints on the 1940s . . . There were battles in the jungles of the Pacific, the sands of North Africa . . .

One might expect that my trip down "memory lane" would end at Blow Gym, when one considers the hours spent there with the basketball team over four memory-filled years. However, when I reflect on my days at William and Mary back in the late '40s, my thoughts revert to friends, classes, magnolia trees, Sunken Garden, Mr. Clark in English, the occasional snow that reminded me of my hometown, Chicago… and the Dogs of Williamsburg.

Yes … the Dogs of Williamsburg! Those ubiquitous, friendly animals that apparently had no homes or masters, but found their way into the hearts of many students.

There was George, a big, burly mixed-breed creature, who was either 60 years old, or was a clone of previous "Georges" because no one dog could have been so well-known by generations of students. He was never seen to eat, but was far from undernourished. God must have watched over George because he always made it across College Corner, even during the busiest of tourist times, and sometimes against traffic. George was there when I arrived on campus … he was there when I left. Years later, my children, who attended my alma mater, often spoke of the "dogs" … possibly including George.

C. F. GIERMAK '50

Willard "Smitty" Smith '44, Joe Markowitz '42, Orville "Arky" Vaughn '43 and I were partaking of a cold brew in pewter mugs at Chowning's Tavern when news of the bombing of Pearl Harbor by the Japanese came over the radio.

Downing our ales in practically one gulp, we descended upon the Duke of Gloucester Street and marched off to the college campus singing, "Good-bye, Mama, we're off to Yokohama."

Arriving at the library (now Tucker Hall), we spread out among the more studious types and announced this momentous event to one and all. Pandemonium, of course, broke loose in that holy of holiest and "school was out" for that day.

It wasn't long after that that the male population of the College of William and Mary became almost non-existent. Off to war we went, faculty and student alike — some never to return. …

My friend and classmate "Smitty" (Willard S. Smith '44) lived down the hall from me in Old Dominion. He came from Detroit with a dozen or so argyle socks that his mother had lovingly knitted for him. Smitty was a classy dresser, in the latest Detroit fashion, but he wasn't very careful of his clothes — especially the argyle socks. After wearing a pair for a day or two he would throw them in the corner and put on a fresh pair, dispensing of those in the same fashion a day or two later. However, he was careful to keep them separated one pair from another. At the end of the month when he ran out of clean socks, he went back to the first discarded pair and started over, working his way through several times until Christmas break. Then he took the entire lot home for his poor mother to wash.

JOHN S. ENTWISLE '44

There was the thrill of sorority rush, making new friends, and exploring new interests and ideas, library dates, the dances in the Sunken Garden with big name bands, late-night bridge games, time-out from studying for a Coke or tin-roof sundae from the Corner Shop, the panic of the first semester exams, and the panic of producing a senior term paper.

There was the privilege of making the varsity basketball team, of working on the *Colonial Echo*, serving as president of Mortar Board, and being a member of the Honor Council.

There were the rains, the boots we all wore, the freshman beanies and beer jackets, the Homecoming parades (how we did work on our Pi Phi floats) and the family and friends from out of town would treat us to a "real" meal at the Travis House, Lodge or, better yet, the Inn.

I, for one, knew little of what was happening in Europe. It was a different world we stepped into as graduating seniors, a world in which we left our innocence behind.

MARGARET MITCHELL
MOLLENKOPF '41

"They're Either Too Young or Too Old" was a popular tune in 1945. It also described precisely the male portion of the freshman class of that year.

World War II had ended just weeks before I enrolled as a freshmen at William and Mary. The intricate process of demobilization had yet to be worked out. Consequently, the handful of male freshmen that year were either fuzzy cheeked youths too young for the draft or older 4Fs.

The College did its part to keep our lives chaste. An intricate set of social rules governed our behavior — women students were not allowed to ride in cars

40

A hellish world war and its aftermath made their imprints on the 1940s. With men going to fight, women worked, often in war industry factories. There were battles in the jungles of the Pacific, the sands of North Africa and the fields of France. Bobbysoxers were in fashion, and slumber parties the rage. The jukebox provided new music. Radio and hits like "Duffy's Tavern" had to cope with television and the likes of Milton Berle. Brooklyn's Jackie Robinson became the first black to make the big leagues.

In Williamsburg, citizens, including the students, took their day and night tours of duty in the bell tower of the Methodist Church spotting aircraft; the USO opened on Duke of Gloucester, and townspeople invited military personnel from nearby bases into their homes for food and hospitality. Camp Peary appeared, and the community of MacGruder vanished. Paul Green's symphonic outdoor drama, "The Common Glory," made its debut in the new Matoaka amphitheater. Dentist "Polly" Stryker became mayor.

At the College Dr. Pomfret succeeded Mr. Bryan as president. The Naval Training School for Chaplains opened in Marshall-Wythe and used Monroe and Old Dominion dorms as well. The Army Specialized Training Unit was created, using Brown and Tyler dormitories. Victory Ships were named James Blair, John Tyler, Botetourt and the U.S.S. William and Mary, and Lord Botetourt was sandbagged. The Institute of Early American History and Culture was founded and President Truman visited.

The tennis team brought home national championships in 1947 and 1948. Coaches Voyles and McCray brought big-time football with two bowl games, and Buster Ramsey was W&M's first team All-American.

Lambert was dean of students and registrar. Katherine Jeffers was dean of women and John Hocutt dean of men. Carl Fehr began to direct the choir; Jess Jackson, William Guy, Charles Marsh, James Miller, Pelzer Wagener, Richard Morton, Warner Moss and Harold Fowler were among students' favorite faculty members. Dr. Swem and Dean Landrum retired.

Women editors abounded as Elizabeth Costenbader became the first female editor of The Flat Hat. *Five other women editors followed in seven years, but separate men's and women's honor councils continued. There was "Duc" Week and its required bowing to Botetourt while big-name bands returned after the war. Midwinters and Spring Finals were primary social events. Clubs, including Backdrop, Amateur Radio, Dramatic, debate, varsity and international relations flourished.*

or go beyond certain town limits without special permission. We could only be out until 10 o'clock on week nights, 11 on weekends. On "Sexless Mondays" the deadline for dating was 7 p.m.; it was on that night that sororities and other clubs held their meetings. Failure to abide by the rules brought disciplinary action from a student-run council.

But there was life beyond the books. The town was crawling with soldiers and sailors from nearby military camps. Somebody could always fix you up with a blind date with a serviceman. Most of the blind dates I accepted turned out pretty well — the guys were far from home and lonely and happy for a little feminine company. In fact, a couple of these dates resulted in a steady relationship, or as steady as the Army or Navy would allow.

What a change 1946 wrought! By then the vast bulk of the men who had served in World War II had been discharged, and the GI Bill enabled many ex-warriors an opportunity to attend college.

All of a sudden William and Mary was overrun with veterans. The athletic programs were revitalized and the fraternities were reactivated. The euphoria of the war's end spilled over onto the campus. The veterans were a different breed from those who had never experienced boot camp and combat — they studied hard, but they also played hard, seemingly making up for lost time. It was an exciting time to be in college.

ELAINE CAMPTON BAKER '49

It was my senior year, just prior to Pearl Harbor, as I recall. Prime Minister Winston Churchill was visiting the campus. I had the honor of escorting him and his entourage from the President's House to the Wren Building for a scheduled tour of that building.

Mr. Churchill's first act upon leaving the President's home was to light up one of his famous foot-long cigars, which he proceeded to savor, leaving billowing clouds of blue smoke in his wake, as we strolled those hundred or so paces.

I would like to say that he and I chatted amiably all along the route. Not so. He was much too preoccupied with enjoying his smoke and — or so it seemed at the time — with counting the bricks beneath his feet. And, for my part, I was much too over-awed with my singular responsibility to even attempt a meaningful conversation.

One thing did *not* occur to me. Nor to anyone else in the entourage. That was that not even the prime minister of England would be permitted to enter the Wren Building with a lighted cigar.

It fell to Henry Billups, the venerable custodian of the building, to step forward at the entrance doors and very politely suggest that he would be most pleased to hold Mr. Churchill's cigar for the duration of the tour.

The cigar was proffered. And a very proud Henry Billups shuffled all the way around the Wren Building with it, arriving just in time to return the treasure to the exiting prime minister.

There was a brief exchange of quiet words between the two, the upshot of which being that Mr. Churchill, sensitive to Henry's uncomfortable role in fulfilling his duty, very graciously suggested that Henry might enjoy keeping that cigar as a memento of their encounter.

Never had I seen a face glow with such pride. Never since his youth, I suspect, had Henry stood so tall.

I was told, subsequently, that practically all in the black community descended on Henry's home to see (and sniff!) his trophy. Dear Henry, already universally loved and deeply respected, had become an overnight legend.

C. MALCOLM SULLIVAN '42

Memories and emotions were magnified by the time we had spent in service to our country during World War II. We had served our country and now we were graduating from the college which had served our country so magnificently over the centuries.

The Wren Building with Lord Botetourt flanked by Brafferton and the President's House formed a perfect setting for graduation from this College filled with beauty and immersed in history.

Seniors and the president's party assembled at the Sunken Garden between the library and Phi Beta Kappa Hall. We could see the buildings which housed science, the administration, mathematics, and so forth. Our undergraduate appointments had been met by crossing and re-crossing the Sunken Garden. All of our College surrounded us for this final farewell.

THOMAS M. MIKULA '48

When I entered William and Mary as a freshman in 1936 as a tall, gangling boy of sixteen, I found myself living in Tyler Hall as the only freshman. All the men in my section of Tyler Hall were upperclassmen, and participated in football or other fall sports. Peace and order was the law of the times since all were on pledge against smoking or drinking.

During these early times, I seemed to have won the opportunity of going down to the Capitol Restaurant to get sandwiches for the guys every night about 11 p.m. I kept wondering why I was lucky enough to draw the short straw for about a month. Finally, I took two straws and I found that all of the straws were the same length. I suddenly found the reason I had been so fortunate.

At my first visit home during Thanksgiving, my dad asked me if there was any drinking in the dorm. I told him that I had not seen anybody drink. After returning from Thanksgiving, I did find things different. My first meeting with Dean Lambert was when he found me under my bed after one of our rowdy evenings. He had visited our floor to make an observation and to quiet down the group. I had crawled under the bunk so that he would not see that I was involved. Things had changed a great deal since training was over and pledges were off.

Who could ever forget the costume Christmas parties given by our president, John Stewart Bryan? Even more exciting were the Finals with all of the big name bands. The dances were held in the Sunken Garden. Great and glorious days.

RAYMOND T. WALLER '40

Dr. Albert DeLisle, a biology professor at William and Mary, was combining a visit to his parents with a recruiting trip, looking for boys to go to college under a work study plan. We later were more commonly known as The War Workers.

On July 12, 1942, I was on a train to Williamsburg, along with six others recruited from the Holyoke, Massachusetts, area.

It might be worth it to note that most of us would never have made it to college because of finances. I arrived in Williamsburg with my brother's only suit (I didn't own one), my brother's clothes, my brother's shoes, which did fit me, and the only family suitcase, which had gone to college with my sister in 1933. My entire amount of money was $5.12 and as frightening as that sounds, when I met some of the older boys who had less than I had, my fears left me.

HARRY TANZER '49

As I stood in line to register for classes in the fall of my freshman year in 1937 at William and Mary, uncertain as to what my schedule should be, the young freshman girl in front of me gave me advice which I took and have never regretted; "Find out who the good professors are and take classes taught by them."

This resulted in my taking one of the best courses any student could ever have, which was called "Introduction to the Arts," taught by Leslie Cheek, who was to go on to be the curator and director for more than twenty years of the Virginia Museum of Art in Richmond, among other things. It consisted of what seemed to me to be hundreds of slides concerning the histories of painting, sculpture and architecture. I nearly failed the course, but I have been forever grateful to him and to other fine professors who opened the eyes of a 17-year-old from Oklahoma to the glories to be found in art.

MARGARET (PEGGY) PECKS LATHAM '41

We share a million memories! Those old familiar faces — Whitey, Tuga, Sally, Al, Edie, Andy — and those everyday activities like sitting on the Sunken Garden steps or the log in front of Taliaferro. We remember the magic of chapel in Wren, convocations in old Phi Bete, and of the Whiffenpoof Song at Chowning's. Etched on our remembrance are those grand ladies, who were the House Mothers — Mrs. Campbell, Mama String, Mrs. Lambeth — quietly watching over us, giving us the benefit of their kindly wisdom. The train or the Greyhound sometimes took us away and brought us back to our small campus, dearly beloved. Somehow we never missed riding in a car. After all, we had just been through the war and now we were home, safe, at William and Mary.

LUCY VENABLE JONES MURPHY '48

I arrived on the campus in September of 1941, a very unsophisticated 17-year-old with a burning ambition to become a second Margaret Bourke-White, the legendary photographer on the staff of *Life* magazine. In order to further this ambition, I tried out for the three college publications: *The Flat Hat*, *The Royalist* literary magazine and the *Colonial Echo*.

The Flat Hat assigned me to take pictures at the Fall Convocation in old Phi Beta Kappa Hall. I arrived there with my camera and gear. In those days flash units were a completely separate apparatus which had to be attached to your camera. Flash bulbs were about the size of ordinary light bulbs, and they made a popping noise when they went off in a burst of blinding light.

I went about my business. When Dean Miller (Dean of the Faculty) went to the lectern, I decided to move in close, crept up to the front intent on the job I was assigned to do, went to step up on what must have been some kind of platform in front of the stage and tripped. I went head first onto the stage with camera, flash unit and flash bulbs bouncing all around me.

I don't remember anything from that moment as I write this more than fifty years later. I did make the staff of each of the publications, and during my junior year was chief campus photographer.

VIRGINIA LEE MCALINDEN '45

As a genuine, born-and-bred Connecticut resident, I was one of the post-bellum students standing on College Corner, shouting at tourist cars from the north, "Yankee Spy!"

"Come to my office at your: a. convenience; b. earliest convenience; c. earliest possible convenience. Dean J. Wilfred Lambert" Wow! What had I done wrong now?

Professor Dr. Warren Moss, stimulating student thought by outrageously scheduling the demise of the Republican Party, charting the drop in votes from 1928 through 1940. Dr. Merrymon — in physics lecture class — showing the pull of gravity on feathers and on rocks. That gracious lady of Virginia — Dean Grace Warren Landrum.

Cary Grant selecting our campus beauties. Finals dances in the Sunken Garden! Hollywood never had such sophistication and glamour! December 7, 1941 — from Kolledge Kids to military within weeks or months.

That "Wonderful Wizard of Ours" — Carl Voyles producing championship football teams — 1939 through 1942. Calling time-outs in intramural athletics to have a soft drink and a cigarette.

Political parties in student politics. Yes, even smoke-filled rooms. Great fun!

MILTON GREENBLATT '43

"Those were the days ... 1937-1941!" Happy memories — they flood the mind! Here are just a few!

The array of excellent professors who challenged all of us to the utmost as we sought an education. The truly historic setting of William and Mary in Williamsburg, between Jamestown, the first settlement, and Yorktown, where Freedom was won. The restoration created by the Rockefeller Foundation to restore the town as it was in the early days as well as improving the old buildings.

The student body, not large in numbers, but small enough that we knew our professors personally and a major portion of the student body individually.

The town and the College were closely intermingled so that it seemed like one large campus — a happy coordination of vibrant people with positive attitudes.

The mix of sports, arts and especially theatre, with people who moved on to major accomplishments in the field after finishing W&M.

The holiday seasons and the big band dances in the Sunken Garden — there were joyful occasions for listening and dancing, including bands such as Les Brown, Hal Kemp and Kay Kyser.

HOUSTON ASHWORTH '41

"I like Ike" dominated the 1950s with the Korean War ending the career of General Douglas MacArthur. Elizabeth II became England's new queen and Elvis Presley was on his way to becoming king of rock 'n' roll.

Neil Hock turned the key in the lock of Monroe 308 as I walked out of Monroe 306 that first day which began the rest of our lives in the fall of 1954.

We nodded hello and I realized I was looking into the eyes of the first friend I was going to have at W&M. Followed by his roommate, Rod Elliott, who was followed by Bob Thomas and his roommate, Tony Wilson, and also Smoky Sherman, who wasn't the roommate of any of us.

The core of my life was forged on that wing of Monroe Third. Me, from Brooklyn, who thought about nothing but show tunes, and five small-town jocks from Pennsylvania, Massachusetts and Virginia. Walking into my room one day and finding it no longer had a door attached to it. Another time not being able to get out of my room to get to a show I was supposed to be in because this gang of mine had fashioned a rope of wire coathangers to keep me locked in. Exploding over all these injustices at Bob Thomas (he was the handiest), who taught me a lesson when he responded indifferently and said, "Well, if we didn't like you, we wouldn't bother." Oh. Neil telling me one day, "Well, you finally did it. You got Bob to major in fine arts." Not exactly true, but I accepted the blame which I took as a compliment.

These guys showed me (whether they knew it or not) how to be tough and independent, while I showed them they had a broader taste in friends than they thought they did. And after two and a half years knowing I must leave them because I had done all the growing I could there. And I had more to go. What I didn't realize was that all I was removing was my body. Large portions of my soul and heart remain in that dim hallway where we are all still eighteen to this day.

PETER NEUFELD '58

My first contact with Dr. William Guy was while I was still in high school and came to William and Mary to compete for a scholarship. On that day I heard a very gentle man, with a wonderful, broad smile, give instructions for the test. Here was the head of the department of chemistry giving words of encouragement, reassuring us, and letting us know that the destination of the world did not depend on our individual performance. No matter whether I won the scholarship or not, I wanted to study under this man.

Dr. Guy taught two major courses and several minor ones. The most amazing thing to me was that he taught Chemistry 101 and 102 on the second floor of Rogers Hall, and then he would walk up to the third floor and teach physical chemistry. During this short walk he immediately transformed his lecture style to a 400 level without breaking stride.

Some of his little techniques to make a point have remained with me throughout the years. I have never misspelled separate since 1950. Whenever I write the word, I always see the way he wrote it on the chalkboard: sepArate. He used these nudges to help thousands of freshmen through the obligatory science requirement. Although one could see that his patience was sometimes taxed to the limit, for example, by people who boiled hydrochloric acid for a water bath, he maintained his composure. A plethoric, red face would occasionally reveal his level of frustration.

His office door was always open and at that time he was also the pre-med adviser. He didn't take this job any more lightly than he took his job as a professor. He accepted more responsibility, as the adviser, than merely to make sure one was taking the correct courses to get into medical school. There was a willingness to discuss the pros and cons of going into medicine or simply to talk about personal problems. When I applied to medical school, he called me into his office for a chat and wanted to know why I was in such a hurry, since I was 18 years old. He convinced me to take a fourth year at William and Mary, relax, and enjoy some free time. I did and it was a wonderful year.

In my mind Dr. William Guy taught me far more than chemistry. He taught me a sense of self-worth, to strive to be a gentle person as well as a gentleman. If I can conclude my life and be loved by people as he was then it will have been a fantastic journey.

WINFRED O'NEIL WARD '54

Feminist rhetoric declares that women students in the 1950s were still being channeled into the MRS degree while men students were being prepared to undertake professional, academic, public service and business careers. Feminists did not know W&M's professors of the 1950s who provided superb guidance to W&M coeds. The

50

"I like Ike" dominated the 1950s with the Korean War ending the career of General Douglas MacArthur. Elizabeth II became England's new queen and Elvis Presley was on his way to becoming king of rock 'n' roll. Marilyn Monroe was a live sex symbol and James Dean a dead movie idol. Drive-in movies were the craze along with Davy Crockett, hula-hoops and poodle-cut hairdos. Television defeated radio, and Senator Joe McCarthy, "I Love Lucy," "American Bandstand" and "Gunsmoke" were TV hits. Martin Luther King began his non-violent movement against segregation.

In Williamsburg, the first shopping center took many favorite businesses from uptown while motels began to replace tourist homes. The post office was in the arcade building. The National Governors' Conference came to town, and the area celebrated the 350th anniversary of the Jamestown Settlement.

At the College, Admiral Chandler replaced Dr. Pomfret as president as a scandal rocked the football program, but the hustling "Iron Indians" brought respectability. Britain's Queen Elizabeth II made an historic visit to her "Royal College" as did President Eisenhower. Phi Beta Kappa Hall burned, and a new auditorium was built where a new campus would soon rise.

Voting was at "Jockey Corner." The library also was a social center and the Ludwell girls regulated their schedules around the "green machine." Lord Botetourt, victim of too many pranks, was removed. Whiskey was a campus mascot. The Colonial Festival began and Homecoming continued to grow. A separate music department was created and the choir and band blossomed.

Don't forget: interest night, illegal cars, WSCGA, ROTC, pep rallies with bonfires, "beatniks," graduation in front of the Wren, the Colony Room, formal dances in Blow Gym, curfews, Danny Campus and Barrett Beach.

John Hocutt and Joe Farrar were deans of men and Dorothea Wyatt and Birdena Donaldson were deans of women. Coaches included Tipton, Freeman, Drewer, Baird and Chambers. Dudley Woodbridge was cited as one of the nation's top professors; G. Glenwood Clark and W. Melville Jones made English enjoyable and Dr. Fowler's Henry VIII lecture already was legendary. Senior faculty included Emily Calkins, Althea Hunt, Donald Southworth, Pelzer Wagener, William Guy, Albion Taylor, Wayne Gibbs and "Pappy" Gooch.

1950s was still a time when requirements for the Ph.D. degree in science included passing reading exams in two foreign languages. Six weeks after entering W&M, in freshman biology lab, Dr. Sohn asked me what language I was taking. I replied, "Scientific French." He then said, "Be sure to take German. You will need it in graduate school." Dr. Sohn's lectures in genetics resulted in my early commitment to that field.

The graduate school track, German, and interest in genetics have paid off in multiple ways. Most immediately at W&M. The Exeter Exchange Scholarship Committee asked me if I was a "secret pre-med." I said, "No." This possibly weighed in my favor in becoming the first undergraduate coed to spend a year at the then University College of the Southwest, Exeter, England as W&M's exchange student in 1952-53.

HENRETTA TRENT BAND '54

It was the late 1940s. World War II was finally over. A sense of optimism swept through America. In Williamsburg, veterans flooded the William and Mary campus. The GI Bill of Rights provided our tuition, books and fees, plus $65 a month living expenses.

Freshmen in those days were required to wear silly-looking Duc caps, or beanies, and bow to the statue of Lord Botetourt, then located outdoors in front of the Wren Building. The College made a special concession to the veterans, excusing us from these "childish" practices. We who had worn the steel helmets of war could not be bothered with Duc caps. We were the hardened veterans. Or were we?

Some of our antics — still vivid after more than forty years — indicate we may not have been the sober and somber men of the world we thought we were. Picture this scene:

We would gather on College Corner at dusk, eight or ten of us on one side of Richmond Road, about the same number on the other side. When a car approached, we bent down in unison as if to pick up a long rope stretched across Richmond Road. Raising up, we would pantomime stretching the non-existent rope across the road, causing motorists to come to a screeching halt, much to the delight of other students hanging out on the corner.

JAMES W. BAKER '51

I was 24 years old when I arrived in Williamsburg as a junior in 1953. I had served two stints in the Army and had worked on the Norfolk waterfront for over a year following my second discharge; thus, my arrival at the College was not my first trip away from home.

The fraternity lodges were available for rental during the summer months. The landlord was the College, not the fraternity. The No Drinking Rule did not apply to those facilities during the summer — or, at least, it was of even less concern than during the academic year. Another, less abominable rule was that only graduate students could rent lodges. During the summer of 1955, I was a graduate student, I was 25 years old, and I drank beer. I rented a lodge for the summer. My roommates were two of my fraternity brothers who were undergraduates and who were working in Williamsburg that summer. They drank beer, too.

There must have been some complaints about us that summer, because when the next summer rolled around, there was a new rule. Only College employees could rent the lodges. In the spring, I had signed a contract to teach Accounting 201 and 202, beginning in the fall. That made me an employee, so I rented another lodge for the summer of 1956. Two different fraternity brothers were my roommates. They also drank beer. We had fun that summer.

WILLIAM T. PRINCE '55

The Ludwell Dorms on Jamestown Road in the '50s had both advantages and disadvantages. The main disadvantage I found was the "Green Bus" system. It was virtually impossible to walk from Ludwell to any class and if you missed the last bus home you were in BIG trouble. As a result, lateness and its penalties became a prime concern to me.

One glorious fall day, having of course missed the proper bus, I found myself madly rushing to my freshman English class in the Wren Building. I was abruptly stopped by a small gathering of rather awesome-looking "older" gentlemen, only one of whom looked remotely familiar. Thinking I had been caught breaking one of the multitudinous restrictions of the era, I immediately mentally panicked. Every possible excuse used by me, my friends or my friends' friends simultaneously flashed through my mind. I did not even notice that the group was focused around an object on rollers which turned out to be a rather elegant sundial set upon a pedestal. A distinguished looking gentleman spoke, asking me what I thought of it. I managed to mutter something nebulous, I was still re-grouping from my initial guilt and major-punishment fears. The same gentleman then asked me what I thought if its location. Breathing a large sigh of relief, I then realized that they were just looking for a proper home for the sundial and I was not in any trouble.

One of my major lifetime problems has always been being too quick to speak before thoroughly evaluating the situation and this was no exception. It took me all of about ten seconds to determine that, though the beautiful tree-lined paths in front of the Wren Chapel were a picturesque setting for almost anything, the entire area was lacking in the one element the sundial needed — direct sun. With all the tact of a late-to-class, now guilt-free freshman, I immediately proceeded to present my dissertation on the virtues of the sun. This I followed with my "proper location for sundials theory," emphasizing that exposure to direct sunlight generally aids a sundial's effectiveness. The group, though polite, started shifting their shoes and I surmised I was no longer needed. Graciously I excused myself realizing that my lateness to class was now more of a problem than I originally thought.

Our little sundial gathering had not, however, gone unnoticed. A group of campus strollers had gathered about fifty feet away, directly across my path. They halted my rush and their spokesperson said something like, "What were you, President Chandler and Mr. Rockefeller doing over there with that THING?" I gasped, then gulped and answered something freshman-like: "Oh, we were just looking for the SUN!" Meanwhile a laser-like illumination flashed through my mind. I suddenly realized just WHO they were that I had been lecturing. I couldn't believe that a lowly freshman, late to class, was giving the College president and the head of Colonial Williamsburg solar advice.

At that point I gave up any idea of attending class and returned to Ludwell on the Green Bus. Later that afternoon I embarked upon a curious, reminiscent walk over to the Wren area. There, beside the front fence, in the SUN, was the newly placed sundial. Sometimes missing the Green Bus had its distinct advantages!

ELAINE ELIAS KAPPEL '55

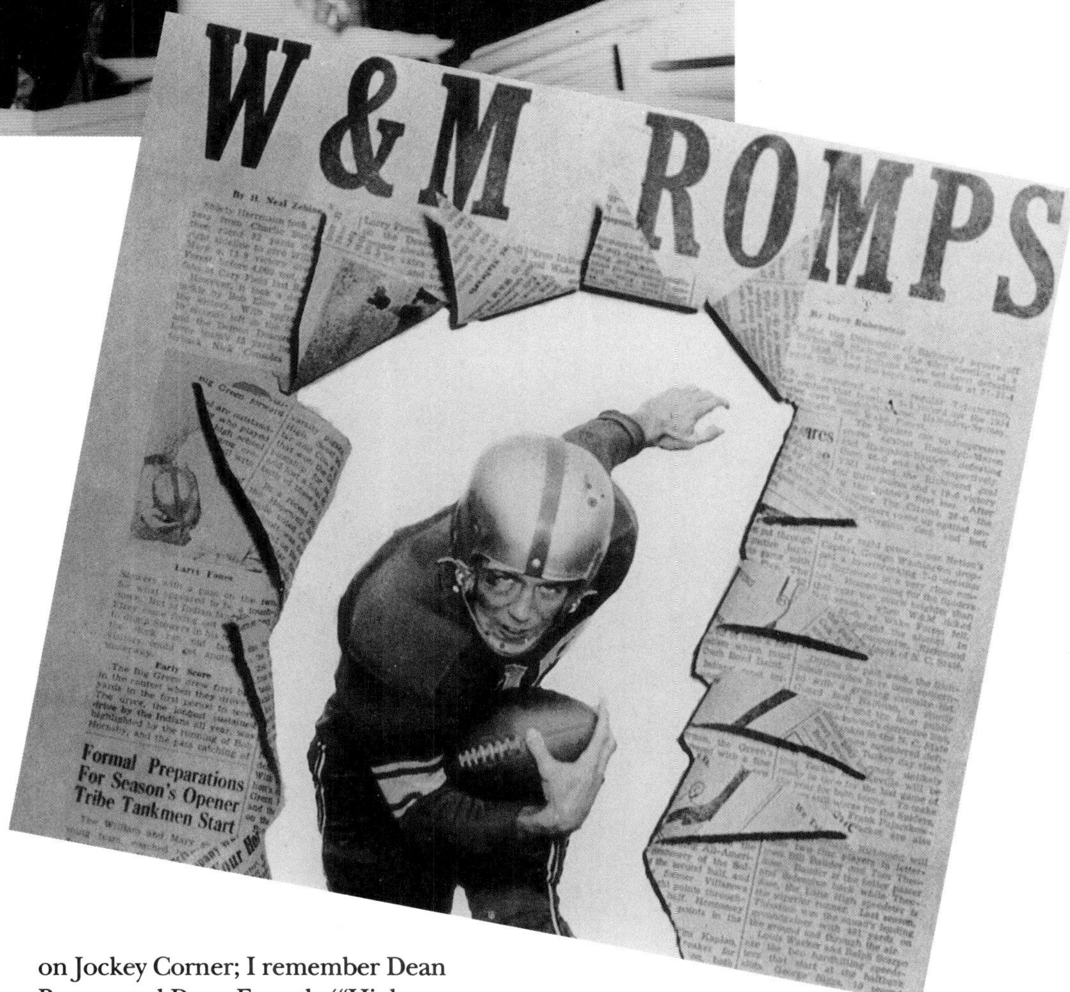

I remember Duc Caps, Priorities and Lord Botetourt; I remember the smell of magnolia blossoms in the spring and the paper factory at West Point; I remember touch football and Frisbee on the grass behind Monroe Dormitory; I remember working in the "Caf," Miss Tinker, Food Fights and the taste of onion in the spring milk; I remember Jockey Corner; Middle Greeks, Corner Greeks, the P.O. and the Flick; I remember the Methodist Church on the corner of DOG Street; I remember Greek Sings and Serenades; I remember panty raids; I remember being introduced to my wife at the Fraternity Lodge, riding on the Green Machine from Ludwell on our first date, getting pinned and engaged; I remember "our" special spot in the Sunken Garden; I remember the CCC Field and intramural football; I remember catching measles during exam period in my sophomore year; I remember President Chandler, Dr. Guy, Dr. McDonald, Dr. McCulley, Dr. Fowler and Prof. Calkins (whose math course I failed to pass three times); I remember campus elections — printing buttons, blotters and pamphlets, hanging oilcloth banners, listening to speeches; I remember pep rallies on Jockey Corner; I remember Dean Barnes and Dean Faquah ("Hi, how you"); I remember the Lambda Chi Alpha All State Ball in Richmond and my wife being selected Virginia Sweetheart of Lambda Chi Alpha; I remember Virginia Beach weekends, especially the one where we were evicted from our hotel in the middle of the night; I remember Monroe Dormitory and Ma Fickland; I remember nickel Cokes, breakfast in the Wigwam and sandwiches from the Deli; I remember chinos, turtleneck sweaters, saddle shoes and black umbrellas; I remember Harry Groves, track meets, shoveling snow off the track to practice, Southern Conference Championships; I remember Wednesday afternoon rote drill and the Drum Bugle Corps.

WARREN P. JOBLIN '60

"Don't let it be forgot that once there was a spot, for one brief shining moment that was known as Camelot."

I grew up at William and Mary. The first thing I learned was to respect and admire "school girls" and "school boys." You don't get to William and Mary unless you're good in school. The second thing I learned was humility. In a sea of "school girls" and "school boys," I couldn't casually backstroke to the finish line. I learned that in some classes treading water was what I needed to do to keep from drowning. Those are important lessons to learn.

My four years at William and Mary taught me to care passionately about the world I live in. The 1960s were scary times in many ways. I remember my anger at the Vietnam War, college protests, sit-ins, trips to Washington to protest. I remember the hush of a hundred young men surrounding the only television set in the Campus Center as we listened for our destiny in the form of numbers in a draft lottery.

I'll never forget a candlelight vigil where hundreds of us sat in the glow of flickering flames crying and mourning the deaths of students killed at Kent State. And always there was music. The songs of Judy Collins, Joan Baez, Bob Dylan, Pete Seeger, and Peter, Paul and Mary are as much tied up with my William and Mary recollections as the Wren Building. I know I joined the Peace Corps as a result of what happened during my four years on campus.

Perhaps the most important lesson I was taught at William and Mary was a reverence for tradition.

RICHARD F. ABRHAMSON '70

That first Sunday reception for freshmen and their parents in 1961 in the Sunken Garden, and Dean Lambert's explanation to the parents, "This place is called the Sunken Garden. It is six inches above sea level and twelve inches above hell " ... then later that first week at Phi Beta Kappa Hall and Dean Lambert saying, "Look at the persons sitting beside you, at least one of you won't be here next year" ... ah, 3.2 beer at the "Corner Greeks" and/or the Cardinal "Puff" game at the Colonial ... Freshman "duc" hats the first two or three weeks of the semester; tipping them to upper class females and/or curtseying to upper classmates! ... "jockeying" on Jockey Corner ... The Queen's Guard Drum and Bugle Corps (I think I was an original member of this corps in the fall of 1961 or at least wore the red tunics, tartan sash and black "bear-fur" hats, first). The Sunset Parade at Homecoming and the melding of past and present ... the William and Mary "Indians," GO BIG GREEN and "Cary Field" ... a flask with my initials on it ... the fraternity lodges and the "classics" played by the "Hot Nuts" (get 'em from the peanut man, ya, ya, ya) ... freshmen women in their dorms by 7 p.m. on weeknights, no shorts for women except for the gym or their dorm ... female curfews in general ... the Ludwell bus ... free passes to the "exhibition buildings" of Colonial Williamsburg and buses free-of-charge ... "all-nighters!" ugh with No-Doze or better? ... Dr. Guy's chemistry class or "learning" English in the oldest, continuously used academic building in America ... The Priorities of the College, especially the Honor System ... the "townies" who had cars ... Tyler A&B and Taliaferro A, B & C, three to a room, nickel six-ounce Coke bottles with names of the town and state where they were bottled on the bottom ... the College bookstore below Taliaferro C where at least five people could shop at the same time ... the student center and cafeteria with nickel coffee, all day bridge games and "match stick" poker games! ... Greek intramural sports and the "All Points Trophy" won by the Pikas in '64, '65 and '66 ... Dudley Jensen in Blow Gym, "directing" athletics and helping us with life ... and those VPI basketball games in Blow with real school spirit raising the rafters, hours before game time ... ROTC house in the basement of Blow with rows and rows of M-1 rifles in their racks ... the chiding from those less fortunate than we as we marched from the Sunken Garden to Phi Beta Kappa parking lot on Wednesday afternoons for drill ... the ROTC Quonset Huts behind the laundry where we learned how great Lee was ... ah, the laundry and twenty pieces per week counting your laundry bag and starched underwear and brown paper wrappings with your clean stuff ... not to forget Trinkle Hall, disease, breaded veal cutlets, mashed potatoes with "saltpeter" added, food fights and sled-riding trays in front of Barrett and Landrum Halls ... and the last of the big panty raids in 1961 when the lights went out ... and in between "jockeying" the stops at Binn's, Frazier-Graves, Casey's, the post office behind the "dirty drug and the "dirty" drug itself ... parents' visits and the trip to Nick's Seafood Restaurant in Yorktown or the Sunday brunch (I don't think we used that term then!) at the Motor House Cafeteria ... Delectable, spicy, greasy chili dogs at Frank's, particularly or only at 2 a.m. Saturday night ... Sorority circle and pledge day ... and those "second class" students who lived in Brown dorm! ... picking up ice for our fraternity/sorority party that Friday afternoon in November at a gas

60 "Don't let it be forgot that once there was a spot, for one brief shining moment that was known as Camelot." John F. Kennedy brought a new touch to the presidency, but two years later it ended on a street in Dallas. The 1960s brought dramatic success for Martin Luther King—"I have a dream,"—and the Civil Rights Movement while weaving a tangled tragedy of war in Vietnam. Hippies, love children, psychedelic, Woodstock, the Beatles, Bob Dylan, long sideburns, "Doctor Zhivago," Huntley-Brinkley, Joe Namath and Arnold Palmer and a walk on the moon.

Colonial Williamsburg opened new exhibition buildings and became one of the nation's tourist meccas as VIPs visited frequently. "Polly" Stryker was mayor; trains still brought students to town but Interstate 64 was unfinished. Drive-in movies prospered and Chowning's offered steaks on the grill and beer inside. Remember Frazier-Graves, the "Dirty" drugstore, "Earl N's," Binn's, Thiemes', Roses, West End Market, Rousso's and Frank's.

Dr. Paschall became president, succeeding Admiral Chandler who became chancellor. The Colleges of William and Mary, a system of five institutions, was created, but lasted only two years. The new campus was begun with Paschall's legislative lobbying efforts. New buildings included Swem Library, Andrews, Millington, Small, Morton, Jones, DuPont, the fraternity complex and a second complex that sororities wouldn't use.

Try to Remember ... Miss Tinker, Dr. Ryan's football Greek, Dr. Moss' political parties, and Ludwell Johnson's Civil War, Dr. Kallos, Dr. Guy, Dr. Fowler, Dean Barnes and Dean Lambert.

The Communist speaker controversy, WCWM, Mermettes, Orchesis, Scabbard and Blade, Old South Ball, Purple Passion, sorority rush acceptance and the dash across Richmond Road and Morris House. The Flat Hat turned 50 and won the Pacemaker Award; Crim Dell was beautified; Spring finals revived; and graduation held under the trees in front of the Wren. Hootenanny, Wampo, Jockey Corner, and the tunnel under Jamestown Road.

Coaches Drewer, Levy and Holtz, "Screaming Joe," "Easy" Ed, and Chambers. Intramurals attracted hundreds in the small confines of Blow Gym. The last panty raid and rain, rain and rain.

Students protested for rights and responsibilities and against the war, in loco parentis and rules about visitation.

station on Richmond highway when the attendant came out and said, "Did you hear the President has been shot in Dallas?" ... a .5 grade point average my first semester, junior year ... calling my parents one week before graduation and telling them "come on down" ... and then the "glorious" and "magical" baccalaureate service and graduate exercises, both in the Wren Courtyard.

CARL RICHARD ("FLASH") WEBER '65

Bucolic setting of the Colonial Parkway as you entered Williamsburg from Yorktown ... Recognition of the pointed shoes worn, indicating my New Jersey roots ... Freshman coach Joe Agee's shrill and intimidating welcome! ... Chaotic registration ... Three in a room (hardly large enough for one) in Dawson House! ... Complexities of keeping a car, illegally ... Requests/demands by fellow Kappa Sig's to use illegal car on a regular basis ... Being blindfolded for eight straight hours, while wearing a tuxedo, during initiation ceremony to Kappa Sigma fraternity in Wren Great Hall ... Keg parties at Gloucester Point ... Cramming for exams ... Dr. Ryan's Ancient Greek classes ... Pat Riley's Education 301 ... John Quinn's essay exam in Accounting 301 ("If you could write about accounting you mastered it.") ... Recognizing ever so slowly that coeds were not to be feared! ... Football weekends ... Assassination of JFK and the somber mood that permeated college life for what seemed like an eternity ... Card games in Tyler annex ... Spring break in Daytona Beach ... "Massive" student protest to influence College administration to allow ABC's Hootenanny show to be filmed on campus ... Final exams ... Losing to West Virginia in final game of '64-65 Southern Conference Basketball Tournament in double overtime ... Virginia Beach ... Graduation Week ... Lifelong friendships.

ROBERT S. ANDRIALIS '65

"Dulcinea" from a new musical about Don Quixote, *Man of La Mancha,* was often sung late at night in a rich, resonant baritone voice coming across the Sunken Garden toward the women's dorms. It seemed to be sung only to me, though I still have no clue about the owner of the voice.

Music is one of my fondest memories of William and Mary. It brought a closely knit group of us together to relax. Mac Henderson '69 and later Jeb Boswell '69 played the piano in the music room. We sang favorites: "Ebb Tide," "Unchained Melody," "Moon River," "Stranger in Paradise," and "This is My Beloved."

On Sunday evenings Father Zung, both professor and priest, hosted Newman dinners at his home on the James River. After a delicious steak dinner, we would gather around his grand piano. He would do the honors, playing while we sang.

Mother said my letters home were filled with Dr. Zung this and Father Zung that. He and I didn't realize it at the time, but we must have fallen in love. A brief courtship after he had left the College for the University of Missouri at Rolla, and we were married.

Seven children owe their existence to God's grace in music. "Dulcinea ... Dulcinea."

NATALIE HILL ZUNG '69

***F**or the class of 1964 it was our senior year. It was Friday afternoon about 1:30, November 22, 1963. I remember where I was, just as each of us remembers that sorrowful, fateful moment in our lives. I was in education math class upstairs in Washington Hall. I don't remember what we were doing at the time because everything suddenly became erased as we heard a voice yelling in the hall, "Kennedy's been shot!" We jolted to attention, looking around one another in disbelief, knowing this must be a joke. The voice cried out again, "President Kennedy is dead!" Everyone was stunned.*

We bolted out of the room, down the three flights of stairs, scattering in all directions to get to the nearest TV set or radio. Within minutes I knew that every student on campus had heard the shocking news. Some ran to the Campus Center, some to their dorms. I ran to the Theta House. As I crossed the Sunken Garden, I remember glancing up at the bell tower of the Wren Building half expecting it to ring—affirming positively that this fateful message was not true. But it didn't ring and I knew the horrible story was true.

I burst into the house and joined my sorority sisters in front of the TV where we all remained for the next 10 hours watching and listening to the unbelievable finality of the events of the day. By that evening it was officially confirmed that John Fitzgerald Kennedy, our 36th president of the United States, had died at 1 p.m. after being shot by an assassin while riding in an open motorcade in Dallas, Texas. We were dazed and speechless.

The next day, Saturday, at noon, the entire college community gathered in Wren Courtyard for a service mourning our fallen hero. Dean of the Faculty W. Melville Jones and Bill Corley, president of the Student Association, led the service in which each of us, with bowed heads personally felt the pain. And it was then that the Wren bell rang true to our hearts confirming our loss.

I look back at my scrapbook of photos, newspaper articles and college memorabilia, and there near the end of the book is the bulletin that *The Flat Hat* issued at 10:45 p.m. on that day. There is the tinted-green photo taken from the Wren steps of the service and a headline: "Let every nation know ... that we shall pay any price, bear any burden ... to assure the survival and success of liberty." There is also a memorial portrait of John F. Kennedy rimmed in black. On the back of the portrait the words remind us—"the trumpet summons us

again … not to bear arms … but to bear the burden of a long twilight struggle, year in and year out, 'rejoicing in hope, patient in tribulation'—a struggle against the common enemies of man: tyranny, poverty, disease and war itself … so let us begin anew." And so we did.

…During freshmen orientation we all had to sign up for the courses of our choice for first semester. …

Needless to say rumors abounded concerning the few classes and professors considered to be "killers." For example, it was well known that economics was the roughest department, and of the sciences you'd better take chemistry because Dr. J. T. Baldwin in the biology department was a tyrant who was out to eliminate freshmen. There was even a sign posted in Jefferson Dorm, "Freshmen, Beware of 'B.'" … I found Dr. Baldwin in the anatomy lab perusing trays of stunned frogs ready for dissection; somehow I couldn't help linking my fate with theirs. … "Miss Peirce, you have already missed two days of my class. If you haven't learned to make up your mind by now, you won't pass biology and you certainly won't graduate." I could feel tears welling up in my eyes. …

Over the course of the year biology wasn't as bad as it might have been. Dr. Baldwin's stern grumblings to me had been a warning, but certainly not a death sentence. … Actually I grew quite fond of Dr. Baldwin. As the year went on he looked more like a grandfather; he was a very proud man, a most informative lecturer and extremely knowledgeable in his field of botany and biology.

… Since biology was the extent of my science requirement, I didn't see much of Dr. Baldwin after my freshman year … only occasionally when I passed by the basement of Washington Hall I'd notice him at a distance diligently digging in his pots and starting more seedlings which he planted all over the campus.

… It was June 7, 1964, our graduation day. I was standing in the commencement line. The department chairs were gathering nearby to lead the processional. Dr. Baldwin caught my eye and came over to me—"I see you made it, Miss Peirce. Congratulations." I was stunned. He even remembered my name after all those years.… I never realized I had made such an impression on him. It was the best commencement ceremony I could ever have imagined!

GINNIE PEIRCE VOLKMAN '64

The Vietnam War ended; the Watergate burglary cover-up finished Nixon's presidency; and the nation celebrated its bicentennial.

Serving as editor of *The Flat Hat* during the 1973-74 school year resulted in a number of fascinating experiences, including the seemingly endless coverage in our arts section of the indomitable Glenn Close, whom we knew as Glennie Wade. Long before critics at *The New York Times* decreed that Glenn was a Broadway sensation, and *Variety* praised her move to the silver screen, *The Flat Hat* predicted that this pupil of Howard Scammon would become a star.

When I think of my senior year, I seldom recall the bell-bottomed pants with huge cuffs, the ties that were almost as wide as the shirts, or the mini-skirts and tank tops that left little to the imagination. But in fact, I do remember what people wore that winter of anything-but-discontent ... absolutely nothing.

The phenomenon of streaking lasted but a week or two. Herds of just-about-naked college men, clad in tennis shoes and sometimes a face-covering stocking cap, ran across the Wren Courtyard, down the sidewalks surrounding the Sunken Gardens, and through the dormitory hallways. They performed this ritual with gusto, under the veil of darkness, but early enough in the evening to ensure a large and enthusiastic audience. They came in all shapes and sizes—streaking had nothing whatsoever to do with fitness—and the only rule was to keep running. (Colliding with those in front or behind could prove embarrassing to all those concerned.)

The grandest streak of all, which involved several hundred rebel-rousers covered with goosebumps from the cold of a winter's night, took place on a Thursday evening around eleven. Our official deadline for Friday's issue of *The Flat Hat* had long passed, but we had reserved the entire front page for streaking photographs, as well as an inside page. With my trusty Canon in hand, I walked from the Campus Center to the Wren Yard and waited, patiently, in the darkness, with an eagle-eye reporter. Her job was to count as accurately as possible the size of the herd—a formidable challenge, because more or less, everyone looked pretty much alike.

Almost simultaneously, we began to hear rumblings from afar. The herd was approaching. Soon the mild rumble turned into a blur of laughter and cheers, and the streakers arrived in all their glory. I wasted little film on the approach, recognizing that even the avant-garde* Flat Hat *would be hard pressed to bring frontal nudity to the masses. But the departure of the herd proved to be acceptably picturesque—no faces or private parts, but more moons than Jupiter in its finest hour.

All the streakers were safe under the covers when we put the paper to bed around 6 a.m., and the pressmen at the *Virginia Gazette* printing plant seemed to especially enjoy this particular issue. What will these kids do next? What did streaking do for circulation? Within minutes after the tidy piles of *Flat Hats* were delivered unceremoniously to the dorms on Friday afternoon, they were gone. A week later, every "extra" issue had escaped *The Flat Hat* office. In fact to this day, I have yet to find a keepsake copy for myself. But never mind. I still have the negatives.

JAMES C. REES '74

Many of my first year memories focus around the dorm. The hallway of Barrett Third East evolved into a common meeting or gathering place. It was there in the hall that we practiced line dances to the beat of Boz Scaggs and Stevie Wonder, anticipating our first campus formals, and waiting for news of sorority bids after rush had concluded. During exams we piled pillows and "husbands" in the hallway, and studied there en masse—seeking reassurance and support from our hall mates to get us through that anxious time. There was a coffee pot plugged in and perking 24 hours a day during exams, and generally a box of cookies or Williamsburg fudge nearby.

All-nighters seemed to be an all-too-frequent occurrence in my first semester freshman schedule—between Wednesday nights at the Pub, fraternity smokers, sorority rush, and the excitement of being away from home, my studies never seemed to be concluded before the wee hours. I can recall too many nights spent ... in the first floor lounges, as we frantically tap-tapped at our typewriters trying to meet the next morning's deadlines for papers. The campus cop on the Barrett beat would frequently stop in to offer words of encouragement and doughnuts.

By spring we had settled down somewhat, and the all-night study sessions were not as frequent. My favorite late-night dorm memory from spring semester is of the Barrett Cotillion, held outside the lawn that April. Who could ever forget the romance of dancing beneath the moon and the stars on a warm Virginia evening?

MARY SOWELL LEAGUE '80

In the spring of 1976 ... I was among the freshmen and sophomore women selected to re-colonize the William and Mary chapter of Phi Mu sorority—a thrill in itself for one's first year on campus. Among the creative activities set for me by my sophomore "Big Sister," Missie Murdock, was completion of an autograph book. At the top of every page of the seemingly endless book she had written a category of person, e.g. lacrosse player, English professor, post office worker, etc. My task was to obtain the autograph of an individual on campus who fit each bill, causing me to blithely accost people all across campus and, happily, to make some new friends in the bargain.

Then I turned to the last page. At the top was written "President Graves." I had to get his signature!

Being determined to complete the book, and with the naive confidence only a freshman could muster, I knocked on the door of the President's House at about 4 o'clock one weekday afternoon. I have no idea what I expected to happen, but there I was. Within seconds of my knock the door was opened by the housekeeper and I, suddenly overcome with embarrassment, gushed out my reason for being there. She asked me to wait in the foyer and disappeared into the house, leaving me to suddenly feel like Pip in *Great Expectations.* The housekeeper reappeared and ushered me into the study where I was at once face-to-face with President Graves. My nervousness and the passing years have erased all memory of what we spoke of, but for a full fifteen minutes Thomas Graves set aside the business of running the College to spend time with an enthusiastic if somewhat obtrusive freshman.

Yes, he signed the book, although in my flustered state it was almost forgotten. He even let me keep the pen with which he signed it. I still have the book, although the pen somehow vanished long ago. But more importantly I have the memory of a brief but meaningful encounter that set the tone for my entire career at William and Mary … four years that taught not only facts and information, but also the value of the individual and the importance of each and every one of us to the life of the College and the world.

Thank you, President Graves.

SUSAN ARNOT HEANEY '79

70

The Vietnam War ended; the Watergate burglary cover-up finished Nixon's presidency; Gerald Ford became the first non-elected president; the nation celebrated its bicentennial; and a Southerner—Jimmy Carter—became president of the United States. The 1970s saw impeachment proceedings against Nixon; anti-war protests and the Kent State shootings; the voting age lowered to 18; assassination attempts on Ford; and the Camp David peace accords. "Bridge over Troubled Water" meant much more; Elton John and "Star Wars" opened an era, while John Wayne, Arthur Fiedler and the Duke of Windsor closed one. Henry Aaron broke Babe Ruth's home run record.

Williamsburg grew as the Merchants Square business area became more oriented to tourists. Charles Longsworth followed longtime college friend Carlisle Humelsine to lead Colonial Williamsburg. Anheuser-Busch's wealth gave James City a tax base by developing a brewery, Busch Gardens and Kingsmill. George's, Parlett Plaks, A&P, Wythe Candy, Suttle's, Massey's thrived and the delis abounded.

William and Mary Hall was opened and the Paschall building boom continued under the presidency of Tom Graves, who brought professional fund raising and a new feeling of the fine arts to the campus. Deans Lambert and Fowler retired and Deans Sadler and Edwards matured. Remember Provost Healy, professors Sutlive, Sanderson, the Donaldsons, the Johnsons, Thompson, MacDonald, Finn, Scammon, Sancetta and Lavach. A new fraternity complex opened; the staid curriculum was revised; the law school got Dean Spong and a new building; and Coach Root and Cary Field weathered a storm: the renewed question of "big time football."

The BSA began to expand its influence; the Women's Dormitory Association ceased while the schools of education and business began to find their way; VARC continued high energy nuclear physics research; the 1972 Colonial Echo *won best in the nation.*

A 1976 presidental debate in Phi Beta Kappa brought national politics up-close as President Ford and Governor Carter and scores of media came to campus. And Emperor Hirohito also visited.

Students were more concerned about others than themselves and activism grew with organizations like Circle K, WATS, the Moritorium Committee, and the political groups. Drugs hit the campus. Women's curfew gave way to coed dorms and "The Common Glory" died. Joggers became active on DOG Street.

The Iran Hostage crisis ushered in the 1980s—the "Reagan Years"—with strong national feelings . . . Communism in the Soviet Union collapsed; Yeltsin succeeded Gorbachev. U.S. troops won the Gulf War.

Something about the natural beauty of the campus as a whole has always filled me with a sense of awe. The wild flowers, the tremendous variety of birds, and the trees—from the flowering dogwoods to the magnificent weeping willows, to the beautiful magnolias—have always helped to make the campus special to me.

I remember one tree in particular which lives in back of Jefferson. When I was a freshman I lived in Barrett and passed that tree almost every day. It was big, with low, sturdy branches. It was the type that invited you to be a kid again and climb it. I did. Whenever the weather cooperated, I'd take my books, a snack and a clock, and climb up into that tree to study and relax.

I have no idea exactly how old it is, but one thing I know for sure is that I am far from the first to climb among its branches. It gives me a feeling of connection to the past, wondering who else in this century and perhaps before walked past that tree, and took the time to marvel at its beauty.

JEANNE LULL HOPKE '80

One controversy ... galvanized the student body during my stay at the College—the 1980 proposal by the athletic department to jump to a "bigger" division, and expand the football stadium. The student body was divided, but the prevailing sentiment appeared to be in opposition, out of fear that beefing up the athletic program would result in lower mean IQ for the campus. The student body prided itself in its collective intellectual ego, and after years of swallowing the story that high marks at W&M were hard-earned due to the policy of "no grade inflation" the apparent willingness of the administration to sacrifice SAT scores for the novelty of a winning football season was a bitter pill to swallow.

"HELL NO, I WON'T GROW" was spray-painted on the wall surrounding the stadium (in the appropriate yellow and green Tribe colors), and in a move that mystifies me to this day, a one-day boycott of classes was organized as a protest. Non-attendance as the best means of objecting to a perceived lowering of academic standards seemed to be oxymoronic to me at the time, but I attended the rally anyway. I can't recall who all the speakers were—one popular philosophy professor whose name escapes me after all these years spoke, and the rally concluded with a rousing chorus of "Let's Expand the Stadium for Christmas." Coverage of the protest was carried in the *Washington Post*, and even *Sports Illustrated*. I have no idea what effect, if any, the protest had on the decision to change divisions; however, I like to believe that the decision to maintain the status quo was a result of the students' voices being heard.

MARY SOWELL LEAGUE '80

Perhaps [my] most unique memory is the time that I served as student liaison to photographer Dan Dry.

Mr. Dry was commissioned by the Alumni Society to put together a picture-book of the College that would serve as a lasting memory for alumni of all ages. My job as student liaison was to introduce Dan to the College from the student's perspective. I was forced to show an outsider what made the College a special place for me, as well as every other student. It forced me to think of the College in a way that I had never thought of it before.

My relationship with Dan quickly turned into a friendship, which definitely made both of our jobs easier. I led him on a general tour of the campus and showed him the familiar scenes of the Sunken Garden, Crim Dell and Lake Matoaka. But the book had to consist of more than familiar places, so he asked me what made the campus unique and, in some sense, peculiar. "Bricks, colonial architecture, the academics, Colonial Williamsburg, the

80 *The Iran hostage crisis ushered in the 1980s—the "Reagan years"—with strong national feelings but a rising national debt. It was the decade of women: first vice-presidential candidate; first on U.S. Supreme Court, first U.S. woman in space. But the ERA effort failed. Exercise became more routine; cable television was strung; and Carson continued "Tonight."*

Fred Astaire, Henry Fonda, Kate Smith, Orson Welles and Grace Kelly died, while Madonna, Bruce Springsteen, Dolly Parton and Michael Jackson blazed new trails and "ET" and "On Golden Pond," made the movies inviting. Andrew Lloyd Webber brought back "The Phantom of the Opera" and Keillor's "Lake Wobegon" turned radios on again. AT&T was broken up; the Statue of Liberty was 100; and there was Donald Trump.

Lieutenant Colonel North was caught up in Iran-Contra; the space shuttle Challenger blew up; and AIDS became a deadly pestilence. Reagan-Gorbachev meetings lessened threats while Lech Walesa's Solidarity foreshadowed the fall of Communism and the USSR.

In Williamsburg world leaders came for the Economic Summit. Scribner's, the Toymaker, Shirley Pewter, Binn's, Beecroft & Bull, R. Bryant, Band Box, High's and Baskin-Robbins nurtured student shoppers. Remember the W&M Restaurant, Beethoven's Inn, College Delly, Blue Rose, Mama Mia's and Paul's Deli? Route 199 came around but businesses lined Richmond Road to the Pottery as outlets sought tourist dollars. Bruce Hornsby, the area's own, hit the music charts.

Royal visitors, the Prince of Wales and Princess Margriet of the Netherlands, came to the College to receive fellowships, while the 200th birthday of the Yorktown battle brought Presidents Reagan and Mitterrand. Joggers and bicyclists crowded streets; lofts were the norm; and intramurals boomed and supper clubs grew. Fire alarms rang but there were still no parking spaces, while the Parkhills and Kappa Sig's "whites" made basketball exciting.

Jefferson Hall burned, Tyler became the Reves Center and old Rogers become old Chancellors which became new Tyler; the Muscarelle Art Museum opened with a colored solar wall; and Trinkle was renovated.

Telecommunications systems put computers into dorm rooms. VIMS became part of the College again. Miss Peebles was the first woman rector in the College's history and alumnus Paul Verkuil succeeded Graves as president. Warren Burger filled the long-vacant chancellor post. Classes in the Sunken Garden. Professors Holmes, Schwartz, Fuchs, Von Baeyer, Heacox, Goodwin were familiar names on campus. Rita Wright was named a MacArthur Fellow. George DeShazo, Jr., became W&M's first Rhodes Scholar.

Coach Laycock brought a second football "golden era" with many winning seasons and a trip to Japan for the Epson-Ivy Bowl while women's athletics gained two national championships: golf in 1981 and gymnastics in 1983.

90 *The Communists in the Soviet Union collapsed as Yeltsin succeeded Gorbachev. U.S. troops won in 100 hours of Desert Storm's Persian Gulf War with Generals Powell and Schwarzkopf leading the way. The savings and loan scandal hit new heights and Judge Clarence Thomas and Anita Hill clashed.*

In Williamsburg tourism was down as a new president took over at Colonial Williamsburg. The Downtown Shortstop and the delis continued to attract students, along with old favorites—Band Box, Massey's, Kinko's and Parlett's.

Renovated old Blow Gym became a "Memorial Hall" for classrooms and offices; a child care center, art studio and graduate dormitory opened and contruction began on a new student center. Tim Sullivan succeeded Paul Verkuil to become the College's 25th president.

William and Mary began to celebrate its 300th birthday and to look toward its fourth century. And the yule log, Homecoming, the Priorities, Lord Botetourt, Spotswood cannon, and, of course, the Wren, were still there.

campus community, and us, the students," was my response. Somehow he grasped my meaning, and today all of these aspects are presented in his book.

Putting together a book is never easy. ... Yet, it was somehow always fun. From having front row seats at Grand Illumination and Yule Log (all courtesy of our press pass), to viewing the campus from a helicopter, to finding two friends who were willing to brave tradition and kiss on Crim Dell bridge (By the way, they are now happily married!), to holding the ceremonial mace, I was making memories, as well as portraying them. Thanks to Dan, I discovered and rediscovered many of the best things about William and Mary. Our collaboration and its end result allowed me to leave a lasting contribution to the College.

Happy 300th Birthday, William and Mary! Thanks for everything you have given me.

JEROME DAVID "J.D." BOWERS II '89

Being at William and Mary was the first time I had spent any significant amount of time outside the great state of Texas. I looked forward to meeting new people, and experiencing life from a new perspective. One of my fondest memories occurred in DuPont Hall freshman year. Three fellow hall mates representing Mechanicsville, Virginia; Long Island, New York; and Pittsburgh, Pennsylvania, along with myself sat up late one night demonstrating how we pronounced certain words or used certain phrases. ...

More important than being at the best school in the country or the incredible education or the beautiful environment and campus that William and Mary provided was the fact that I fell in love during my senior year! Julie Devish has changed my life. My senior year would have been much less memorable without her being a major part of it.

STEWART A. TATEM '89

It was my junior year, so far from home, school, and all that I'd known, when his postcard came. I was studying in Bath, England, while he was enrolled at St. Patrick's in Ireland. We did not know each other very well, but school was our common link. He invited me to cross the Irish Channel and spend the holiday weekend.

I took the train to Holyhead where I caught the ferry to Dun Laoghaire then a bus to Maynooth. ... We were happy to see one another, to grasp something familiar from an alien place. ... And then I noticed his hat, a ragged William and Mary baseball cap, an anachronism there, a tribute to what we loved and shared of home. I don't intend to attach undue symbolic importance to a mere hat, but it did spark something, transcendent of reason, in both of us. Soon he was plying me for news of school, so eager and excited to go over the most seemingly trivial of details and anecdotes from campus. He even produced a worn and yellowed newsletter from the Reves Center, a document which he had apparently read over and over again, searching for comfort and familiarity within its paragraphs.

We decided to go to Cork City, for the great jazz festival. ... In the morning we slipped out into the crisp air ... We weren't quite certain where we were, but we set off down a narrow lane. When it rained we could only laugh at our own predicament, trudging as we were through a beautiful landscape. We talked more of school—football games and classes and endless nights—realizing how much we missed it but also reveling in our willingness to defy reason, to tramp in winter rain with all the time in the world, knowing that youth must be something like this.

ANDREW J. MADIGAN '91

My memories of William and Mary are just like yours—four years of good luck and hard times, academic pressure and Mom's washing machine, old knowledge and young ideas, romance, breaking up, cartoons and world peace, laughter and tears, best friend, bestest friends and falling in love. Even though we each borrowed William and Mary at different times in its history, we all experienced its greatness—the quality of the academic standards, the beauty of the historic campus and the richness of the collegiate life William and Mary offers its students. Our experiences shaped and reshaped the College and primed it for future alumni to be able to take their diplomas in one hand and their beautiful memories of their William and Mary days in their hearts like we did. What a great tradition!

LISA BETH FLECHNER '90

George's
Restaurant
ABC
ON/OFF
ABC ON and OFF George's

Photo Captions and Credits

Jacket. "Old Spotswood" cannon, Wren Yard, *by Lyle Rosbotham '71*

3. Decorative cover on *The Charter, and Statutes, of The College of William and Mary, in Virginia* located in Swem Library, *by C. James Gleason*

5. Stairway in Wren Building, *by C. James Gleason*

6. Rear view of Wren Building, *by William K. Geiger '77*

8-9. Presidents of William and Mary, Davis Y. Paschall '32 (1960-71), Thomas A. Graves, Jr. (1971-1985), Paul R. Verkuil '61 (1985-91) and Timothy J. Sullivan '66 (1992-), *by Tony Sylvestro*

10. Top, portrait of James Blair, first president of William and Mary, *from Muscarelle Museum of Art*

10. Bottom, view of cannon in front of Wren Building, *by Jean Wyckoff Gwaltney '56*

11. Lewis Cohen, professor of fine arts at William and Mary, preparing Tercentenary statue of James Blair, *by C. James Gleason*

12. Left, Homecoming representatives, *by C. James Gleason*

13. Homecoming scene with balloons, 1989, *by Tim Wright*

12-13. Homecoming Parade, 1989, *by Tim Wright*

14-15. Alumni Band at Homecoming, 1989, *by Tim Wright*

16. Top, Dr. Milton Salasky '31 and Frances Spindle Harris '34, *by Tim Wright*

16. Bottom, Phi Beta Kappa key, *by C. James Gleason*

17. Hands holding Olde Guarde Medallion, *by Tim Wright*

18-19. Crim Dell, *by C. James Gleason*

20. Nancy '62 and Bonnie '92 Joblin at Commencement, *by C. James Gleason*

20. Women graduates at Commencment 1992, *by Carol Glover*

21. Field Hockey at Barksdale Field, *by C. James Gleason*

22-23. William and Mary cheerleaders, *by C. James Gleason*

24. Top, Choir on European tour, *by Barbara Ball*

24. Bottom, William and Mary Marching Band, *by Dan Dry*

25. William and Mary Choir, *by C. James Gleason*

26. Top, portrait of King William III and Queen Mary II, *by C. James Gleason*

26. Bottom, statue of Lord Botetourt, *by C. James Gleason*

27. Queen's Guard, *by Dan Dry*

28-29. Wren classroom, *by C. James Gleason*

30. Top, William and Mary baseball player, *by Ken Bennett '87*

31. Bottom, Busch Field, *by C. James Gleason*

30-31. Zable Stadium/Cary Field, *by C. James Gleason*

32-33. William and Mary Theatre, Howard Scammon '34, Richard Palmer, Louis Catron, *by C. James Gleason*

34-35. John Keinath (left) and Jack Musick with sea turtle at Virginia Institute of Marine Science, *by C. James Gleason*

36. Top, window in Great Hall of Wren Building

36. Coat of Arms, *by Dan Dry*

37. Christopher Wren stained glass window at Marshall-Wythe School of Law, *by C. James Gleason*

38-39. Lake Matoaka with students, *by C. James Gleason*

38. Left, carvings in tree, *by C. James Gleason*

39. Statues near Crim Dell, *by C. James Gleason*

40. Top, John Graham '92 and Laura Flippin '92 with College Mace at 1992 Commencement, *by Carol Glover*

40. Bottom, Priorities tablet in rear portico of Wren Building, *by C. James Gleason*

41. Mace, *by C. James Gleason*

42. Top, Great Hall in Wren Building, *by C. James Gleason*

42. Bottom, students outside Campus Center, *by C. James Gleason*

43. Order of the White Jacket members in Great Hall: (l. to r.) Howard Smith '43, Marguerite Huff Brown '54, Jim Anthony '52, Maxey Davis '39, Jim Kelly '51, *by C. James Gleason*

44-45. Yule Log, *by Dan Dry*

46. President's House, *by C. James Gleason*

46. Wren Cupola, *by C. James Gleason*

47. Brafferton, *by C. James Gleason*

48-49. Sunken Garden, *by C. James Gleason*

50-51. Alumni Homecoming Dance, 1991, *by C. James Gleason*

50. Alumni House, *by Tony Sylvestro*

51. 1928 red car in Homecoming Parade, *by C. James Gleason*

52. Top, Sundial, *by Dan Dry*

52. Bottom, Commencement walk over Crim Dell, *by Carol Glover*

53. Commencement, *by C. James Gleason*

54-55. Running in Wren Yard, *by C. James Gleason*

56-83. Photographs from *M. Carl Andrews '27, Agnes '31 and Davis Y. Paschall '32, Wilford Kale '66, W. Samuel Sadler '64, the Society of the Alumni, the archives of the Earl Gregg Swem Library, the* William and Mary News *and the* Colonial Echo.